Giant Panda

Did You Know?

- Only 1,000 giant pandas exist in the wild. Only 60 live in zoos around the world.

- Wild giant pandas live in central and western China.

- Giant pandas live in cold forests and are good tree climbers.

- Giant pandas feed mostly on bamboo but will also eat flowers, grasses, vines, green corn, honey, and even rodents.

CALIFORNIA
Science

Macmillan
McGraw-Hill

Program Authors

Dr. Jay K. Hackett
Professor Emeritus of Earth Sciences
University of Northern Colorado

Dr. Richard H. Moyer
Professor of Science Education and Natural
  Sciences
University of Michigan–Dearborn

Dr. JoAnne Vasquez
Elementary Science Education Consultant
NSTA Past President
Member, National Science Board
  and NASA Education Board

Mulugheta Teferi, M.A.
Principal, Gateway Middle School
St. Louis Public Schools
St. Louis, MO

Dinah Zike, M.Ed.
Dinah Might Adventures LP
San Antonio, TX

Kathryn LeRoy, M.S.
Executive Director
Division of Mathematics and Science Education
Miami-Dade County Public Schools, FL

Dr. Dorothy J.T. Terman
Science Curriculum Development Consultant
Former K–12 Science and Mathematics Coordinator
Irvine Unified School District, CA

Dr. Gerald F. Wheeler
Executive Director
National Science Teachers Association

Bank Street College of Education
New York, NY

Contributing Authors

Dr. Sally Ride
Sally Ride Science
San Diego, CA

Lucille Villegas Barrera, M.Ed.
Elementary Science Supervisor
Houston Independent School District
Houston, TX

Dr. Stephen F. Cunha
Professor of Geography
Humboldt State University
Arcata, CA

**American Museum
of Natural History**
New York, NY

Contributing Writer

Ellen Grace, M.S.
Consultant
Albuquerque, NM

The American Museum of Natural History in New York City is one of the world's preeminent scientific, educational, and cultural institutions, with a global mission to explore and interpret human cultures and the natural world through scientific research, education, and exhibitions. Each year the Museum welcomes around four million visitors, including 500,000 schoolchildren in organized field trips. It provides professional development activities for thousands of teachers; hundreds of public programs that serve audiences ranging from preschoolers to seniors; and an array of learning and teaching resources for use in homes, schools, and community-based settings. Visit www.amnh. org for online resources.

 Students with print disabilities may be eligible to obtain an accessible, audio version of the pupil edition of this textbook. Please call Recording for the Blind & Dyslexic at 1-800-221-4792 for complete information.

B

The McGraw·Hill Companies

**Macmillan
McGraw-Hill**

Published by Macmillan/McGraw-Hill, of McGraw-Hill Education, a division of The McGraw-Hill Companies, Inc., Two Penn Plaza, New York, New York 10121.

Science Content Standards for California Public Schools reproduced by permission, California Department of Education, CDE Press, 1430 N Street, Suite 3207, Sacramento, CA 95814.

FOLDABLES is a trademark of The McGraw-Hill Companies, Inc.

Printed in the United States of America

ISBN 0-02-284375-2/1

3 4 5 6 7 8 9 (071/055) 10 09 08 07

Scientific Method

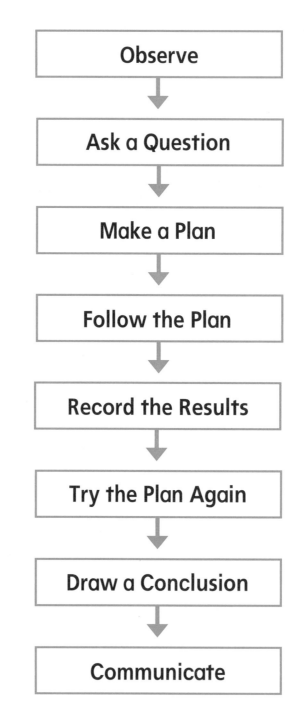

Observe

↓

Ask a Question

↓

Make a Plan

↓

Follow the Plan

↓

Record the Results

↓

Try the Plan Again

↓

Draw a Conclusion

↓

Communicate

Be a Scientist

These children are using
the scientific method. ▶

Life Science

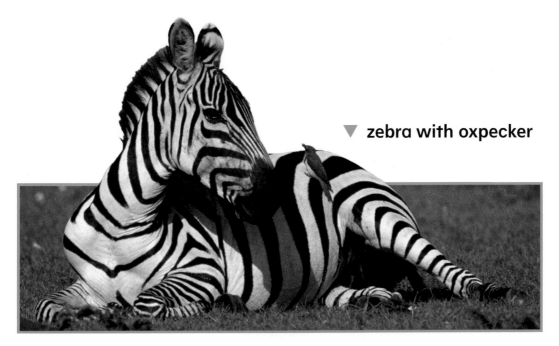

▼ zebra with oxpecker

Earth Science

weather tools

▼ aspens in fall

Physical Science

A toy bear is
solid matter. ▶

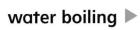

water boiling ▶

Activities

Life Science

Earth Science

These children are using a rain gauge. ▶

Activities

Physical Science

A balance scale
can be used to
measure mass. ▶

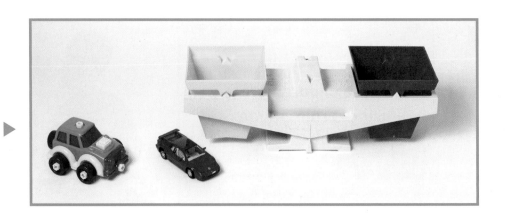

Reference

◄ These children are using thermometers.

Safety Tips

When you see ⚠️ **Be Careful, follow the safety rules.**

Tell your teacher about accidents and spills right away.

Be careful with sharp objects and glass.

Wear goggles when you are told to.

Wash your hands after each activity.

Keep your workplace neat. Clean up when you are done.

Be a Scientist

A ladybug eats tiny insects on a flower.

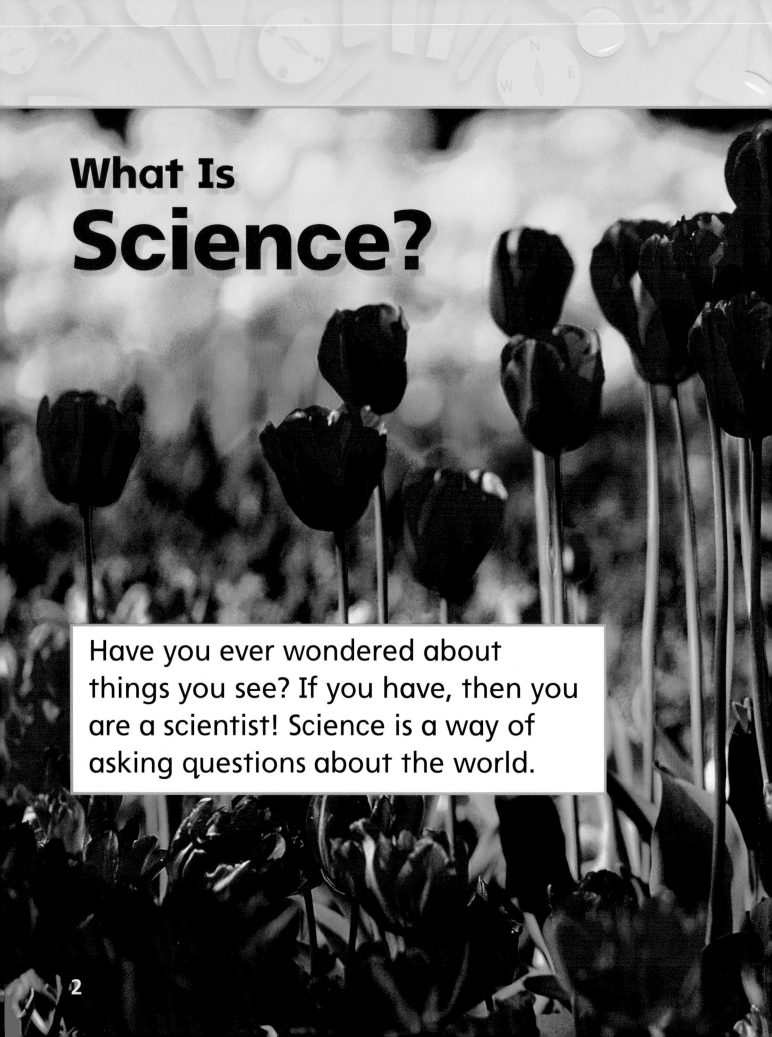

What Is Science?

Have you ever wondered about things you see? If you have, then you are a scientist! Science is a way of asking questions about the world.

Investigation and Experimentation

4. Scientific progress is made by asking meaningful questions and conducting careful investigations. As a basis for understanding this concept and addressing the content in the other three strands, students should develop their own questions and perform investigations. Students will:

a. Draw pictures that portray some features of the thing being described.

b. Record observations and data with pictures, numbers, or written statements.

c. Record observations on a bar graph.

d. Describe the relative position of objects by using two references (e.g., above and next to, below and left of).

e. Make new observations when discrepancies exist between two descriptions of the same object or phenomenon.

Scientists use skills to answer questions about the world. Here are some skills they use.

observe

predict

communicate

measure

put things in order

compare

classify

record data

draw conclusions

Observe

Observe means to find out information. When you observe something, you carefully look, listen, taste, touch, or smell it.

Scientists **observe**. Look at the picture. Can you find something hiding on the leaves?

 I IE 4.d. Describe the relative position of objects by using two references (e.g., above and next to, below and left of).

5

Predict

Scientists **predict**.

What time of year do you think this picture was taken?

What might happen to the trees when the weather gets colder?

Predict means to use what you know to tell what will happen.

Communicate

Communicate means to write, draw, or tell your ideas to others.

Scientists **communicate** their ideas.

Draw a picture of what the trees will look like in cold weather.

I IE 4.a. Draw pictures that portray some features of the thing being described.

Measure

poppy

Measure means to find out how far something moves, or how long, how much, or how warm something is.

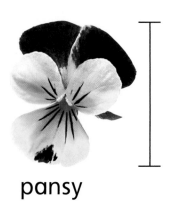

pansy

daisy

Scientists **measure**.

You can measure, too.
Find out which flower is the smallest.
Which one is the largest?

I IE 4.b. Record observations and data with pictures, numbers, or written statements.

Puts Things in Order

Put things in order means to decide which comes first, next, and last.

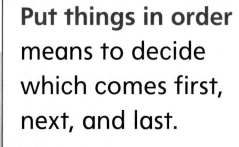

Scientists **put things in order.**

Put the flowers in order from largest to smallest.

9

Compare

Scientists **compare**.

Look at the pictures.
How are the flowers alike?
How are they different?

Inquiry Skill

Compare means to see how things are alike and different.

iris

daffodil

lilac

10

Classify

Scientists **classify.**

Put these flowers into groups that are alike.

Classify means to group things that are alike.

orchid

gladiolus

11

Scientific Method

Scientists ask questions about the things they see. They make a plan to help them find answers to their questions. You can use this plan, too.

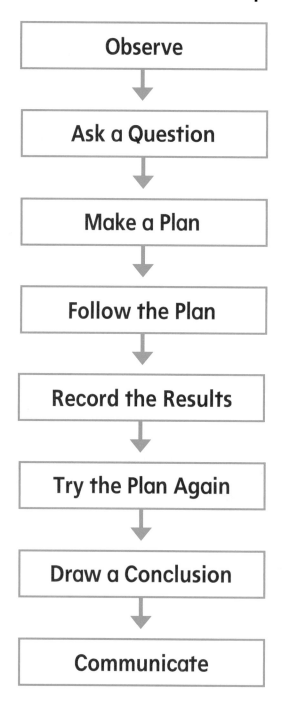

Observe

↓

Ask a Question

↓

Make a Plan

↓

Follow the Plan

↓

Record the Results

↓

Try the Plan Again

↓

Draw a Conclusion

↓

Communicate

Observe and Ask a Question

Scientists **observe** and **ask questions**.

Make a Plan

Scientists make a plan.

Our Plan

1. Get two plants. Measure how tall the plants are.

2. Put one plant in the sun. Put the other plant in the dark.

3. Water both plants with the same amount of water every day.

4. Observe both plants every day. Measure the plants to see how much they grow.

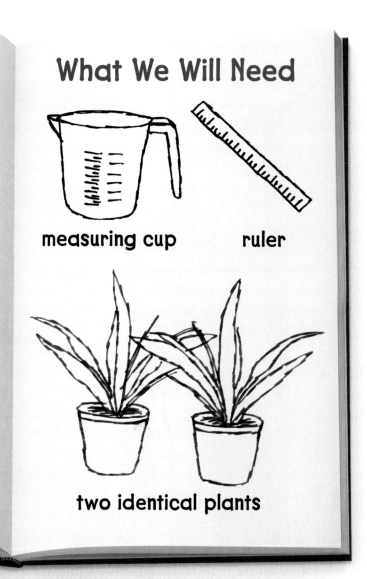

What We Will Need

measuring cup   ruler

two identical plants

1 IE 4.a. Draw pictures that portray some features of the thing being described.

Follow the Plan

Scientists follow a plan.

NO LIGHT

LIGHT

Record Data

Scientists **record** data.

	How tall is the plant that is in the sun?	How tall is the plant that is in the dark?
Week 1	20 centimeters	20 centimeters
Week 2	22 centimeters	20 centimeters
Week 3	25 centimeters	20 centimeters

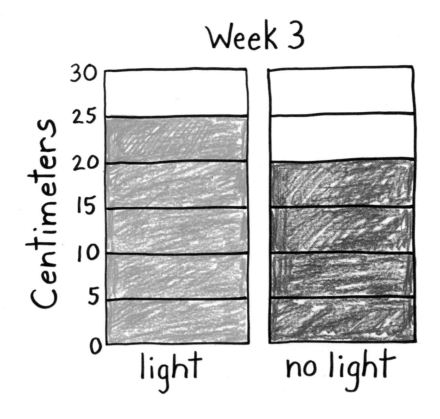

Week 3

1 IE 4.b. Record observations and data with pictures, numbers, or written statements • 1 IE 4.c. Record observations on a bar graph.

Try the Plan Again

Scientists **try the plan again.**
Then they compare their results.

LIGHT

NO LIGHT

I IE 4.e. Make new observations when discrepancies exist between two descriptions of the same object or phenomenon.

Draw a Conclusion and Communicate

Scientists **draw conclusions** and **communicate** their results.

Life Science

Sheep stomachs have four parts.

Plants and Their Needs

 What are plants?

California poppies near the coast

1 LS 2. Plants and animals meet their needs in different ways.

Literature
Poem

ELA R I.2.0. Students read and understand grade-level-appropriate material.

22

Tommy

by Gwendolyn Brooks

I put a seed into the ground
And said, "I'll watch it grow."
I watered it and cared for it
As well as I could know.

One day I walked in my back yard,
And oh, what did I see!
My seed had popped itself right out,
Without consulting me.

Talk About It

Have you ever planted a seed? What happened?

Plants Everywhere

Look and Wonder

Plants grow in all shapes and sizes. What kinds of plants have you seen?

 1 LS 2.a. Students know different plants and animals inhabit different kinds of environments and have external features that help them thrive in different kinds of places.

How are plants different?

What to Do

1. **Observe.** Find some plants around your school. How many different plants can you find?

2. **Record Data.** Draw two different plants that you find.

3. **Compare.** How are the plants alike? How are they different?

Explore More

4. **Communicate.** How could you find out more about the plants you saw?

You need

paper

crayons

Step 2

 I IE 4.b. Record observations and data with pictures, numbers, or written statements.

Vocabulary

plants
habitat

What are plants?

Just like you, **plants** are living things. Living things grow and change. Seeds from plants grow into new plants. The seeds will make a new plant that looks like the parent plant.

▲ Sometimes people grow plants near their homes.

Not all plants look the same. Some plants are very tall. Other plants, like grass, spread out along the ground. Some plants have colorful flowers.

✓ How are plants like you? How are they different?

Redwood National Park, California

Read a Photo

How do you know the trees are tall?

Where do plants live?

Plants live almost everywhere on Earth. They have parts that help them live in different habitats. A **habitat** is the place where plants get what they need to live.

▼ Many desert plants have thick skin and spines to help them live in hot, dry places.

Joshua Tree National Park, California

Rainforest habitats are very wet. Many rainforest plants have leaves that help them live in wet places.

✔ Can a rainforest plant live in a desert?

▶ **Rainforest plants grow tall to get sunlight.**

Think, Talk, and Write

1. **Find Main Idea and Details.** Why can plants grow in different places?

2. Write about a plant near school.

Social Studies Link

Where do plants grow in your area? How would you describe their habitat?

Observe

You use your senses to **observe**.
You can see, hear, taste, touch,
or smell to find out about things.

Learn It

Amy wrote what she observed
about a rose in this chart.

Rose	
See	The rose is red.
touch	The flower is smooth.
Smell	The rose smells sweet.

  I IE 4.b. Record observations and data with pictures, numbers, or written statements.

Try It

Observe a plant.

1. What shape are the plant's leaves?

2. What does the plant feel like?

3. Make a chart like Amy's. Fill in the chart with what you observed.

What Plants Need

Look and Wonder

How are these plants getting what they need to live?

 I LS 2.b. Students know both plants and animals need water, animals need food, and plants need light.

What happens if a plant does not get water?

You need

two labeled plants

water

What to Do

① Place both plants in a sunny place. Water only one of the plants.

② **Predict.** What will happen to each plant?

③ **Observe.** Watch your plants for a week.

Explore More

④ **Infer.** What would happen if the plants got salty water?

 I IE 4.e. Make new observations when discrepancies exist between two descriptions of the same object or phenomenon.

Step ①

Vocabulary

energy

SCIENCE QUEST Explore the needs of plants with the Junior Rangers.

Do all plants need the same things to grow?

Plants need water, air, space, and sunlight to live and grow. Some plants need a warm place with a lot of sun to grow. Other plants grow in cooler places.

oranges

orange trees

Some plants need a lot of water to grow. Rice plants have stems that help them grow in wet places.

rice grains

✔ Do oranges and rice need the same things to grow?

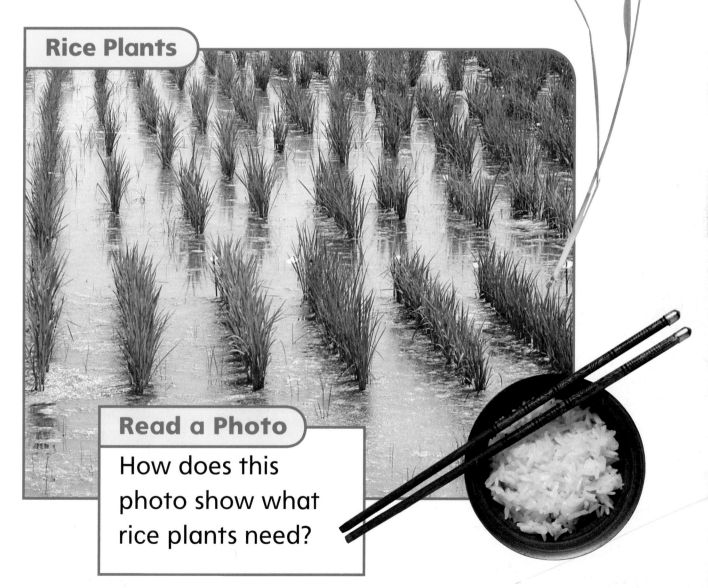

Rice Plants

Read a Photo

How does this photo show what rice plants need?

How do plants use sunlight?

All living things need energy to live and grow. **Energy** gives plants and animals the power to do things. People eat food to get energy. Plants use sunlight to make the food they need.

◄ **Sunflowers turn to face the Sun.**

Plants grow toward the Sun to help them make food. Some plants need a lot of sunlight to grow. Other plants can grow with only a little sunlight.

✔ How do you get the energy you need to live and grow?

Redwood Park, Arcata, California

Think, Talk, and Write

1. **Find Main Idea and Details.** What do plants need to live?

2. Write about different places plants live.

Health Link

Write a story about what you can do with the energy you get from food.

LOG ON e-Review Summaries and quizzes online @ www.macmillanmh.com

Strawberry Fields

Would you like to grow strawberries? The Southern California coast has everything this fruit needs to grow.

Strawberries need warm, sunny days and cool nights. They need a good amount of water and grow best in sandy soil.

That is why more strawberries are grown in California than in any other state.

 ELA R I.2.0. Students read and understand grade-level-appropriate material.

Talk About It

Find Main Idea and Details.
What do strawberry plants
need to help them grow?

LOG ON **e-Journal** Write about it online
@ **www.macmillanmh.com**

strawberry fields,
Watsonville, California

AMERICAN
MUSEUM OF
NATURAL
HISTORY

Be a Scientist

You need

plant

black paper

paper clips

Do leaves need sunlight to stay green?

Find out what happens when leaves get different amounts of sunlight.

What to Do

① Cover three leaves with black paper. Put the plant in a sunny place for a week.

Step ①

② **Predict.** What will happen to the leaves?

 I IE 4.e. Make new observations when discrepancies exist between two descriptions of the same object or phenomenon.

③ **Observe.** Take the paper off the leaves. Do the leaves look like you predicted?

Step ③

④ **Communicate.** What happened to the leaves? Why?

Investigate More

Predict. What would happen to the leaves if you put the plant in a dark place for a week?

Parts of Plants

Look and Wonder

Why does this tree not fall over?
What is holding it in place?

 I LS 2.e. Students know roots are associated with the intake of water and soil nutrients and green leaves are associated with making food from sunlight.

Why does grass need roots?

What to Do

1. Gently pull the grass away from the soil.

2. **Observe.** Use a hand lens to look at the roots.

3. **Communicate.** Draw a picture of the grass and its roots. Describe the roots.

Explore More

4. **Infer.** Do you think roots grow? Why?

 I IE 4.a. Draw pictures that portray some features of the thing being described.

You need

grass in soil

hand lens

Step **1**

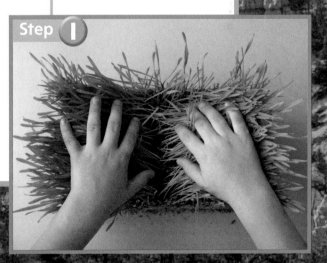

Vocabulary

leaves

roots

nutrients

What are the parts of a plant?

Plants have parts to help them get what they need. **Leaves** use sunlight and air to make food. Water and food move through the stem of the plant.

Some plants have flowers and some flowers grow into fruit. Fruits have seeds. Seeds grow into new plants.

✔ How do plants get their food?

seed

fruit

Strawberry Plant

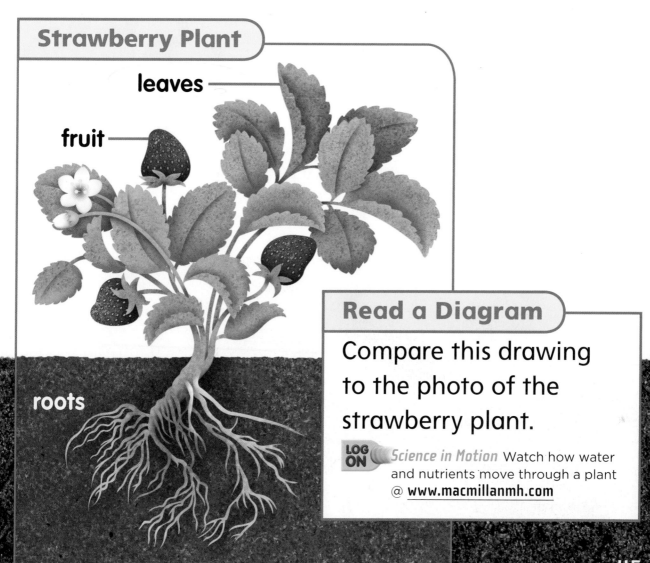

leaves

fruit

roots

Read a Diagram

Compare this drawing to the photo of the strawberry plant.

LOG ON *Science in Motion* Watch how water and nutrients move through a plant @ **www.macmillanmh.com**

What do roots do?

A plant's **roots** take in water and nutrients from the soil. **Nutrients** help the plant grow. Roots also help plants stay in the ground.

Some plants have long and deep roots. Other plants have roots that spread out under the ground.

 Why do plants have roots?

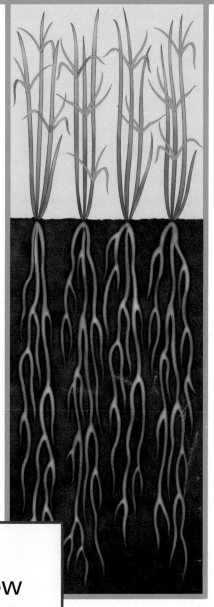

long and deep roots

roots near to the ground

Think, Talk, and Write

1. **Find Main Idea and Details.** How do roots and leaves help a plant?

2. Write about and draw how water and food move through a plant.

Health Link

What are some plant parts you eat?

GENERAL SHERMAN

Meet General Sherman

A tree named General Sherman in California's Sequoia National Park is said to be the largest in the world. It is 275 feet tall. That is as tall as a building with 27 stories!

 Write About It
Write about a tall plant that you have seen. Draw it and label its parts.

Remember
Use words that describe the plant.

LOG ON e-Journal Write about it online @ www.macmillanmh.com

 ELA W I.I.2. Use descriptive words when writing.

Seeds of All Sorts!

Michael sorted his seeds. He made a picture graph to show how many of each seed he has.

Michael's Seeds	
beans	
sunflower seeds	
corn kernels	
peas	

Read a Graph

Does Michael have more sunflower seeds or beans in his collection? If he found 6 more beans, how many would he have? Write a number sentence to show how you know.

Remember
A picture graph helps you solve a problem.

 MA SDAP I.I.2. Represent and compare data (e.g., largest, smallest, most often, least often) by using pictures, bar graphs, tally charts, and picture graphs.

My Plant Book

Some roots are thick.
Some roots are thin.

Some stems are thick.
Some stems are thin.

Some fruits are red.

Some fruits are yellow.

Some seeds have spots.

Some seeds do not.

Some leaves are little.
Some leaves are big.

flower

leaf

stem

roots

Plants have many parts.
But what are their names?

Vocabulary

habitat, page 28

energy, page 36

roots, page 46

plant, page 26

What does each picture show?

1

I LS 2.a

2

I LS 2.e

Complete each sentence.

3. The place where plants get what they need to live is called their

_____. I LS 2.a

4. Plants get _____ from sunlight. I LS 2.b

5. How do plants get their food? I LS 2.e

6. **Observe.** Look at the picture. How are these plants meeting their needs? I LS 2.b

7. **Find Main Idea and Details.** What are the parts of a plant? I LS 2.e

 What are plants? I LS 2

CHAPTER I

Grow a Plant

Plant seeds in soil.

▶ What do these seeds need to grow?

▶ Explain what you need to do to take care of the plant.

▶ Draw a picture of your plant and label the parts.

I LS 2.b. Students know both plants and animals need water, animals need food, and plants need light.

1 The place where plants meet their needs is called a _____. I LS 2.a

A energy

B habitat

C sunlight

D fruit

2 Use the diagram to answer the question.

Which plant part uses sunlight and air to make food? I LS 2.e

A leaf

B seed

C flower

D root

CHAPTER 2

Animals and Their Needs

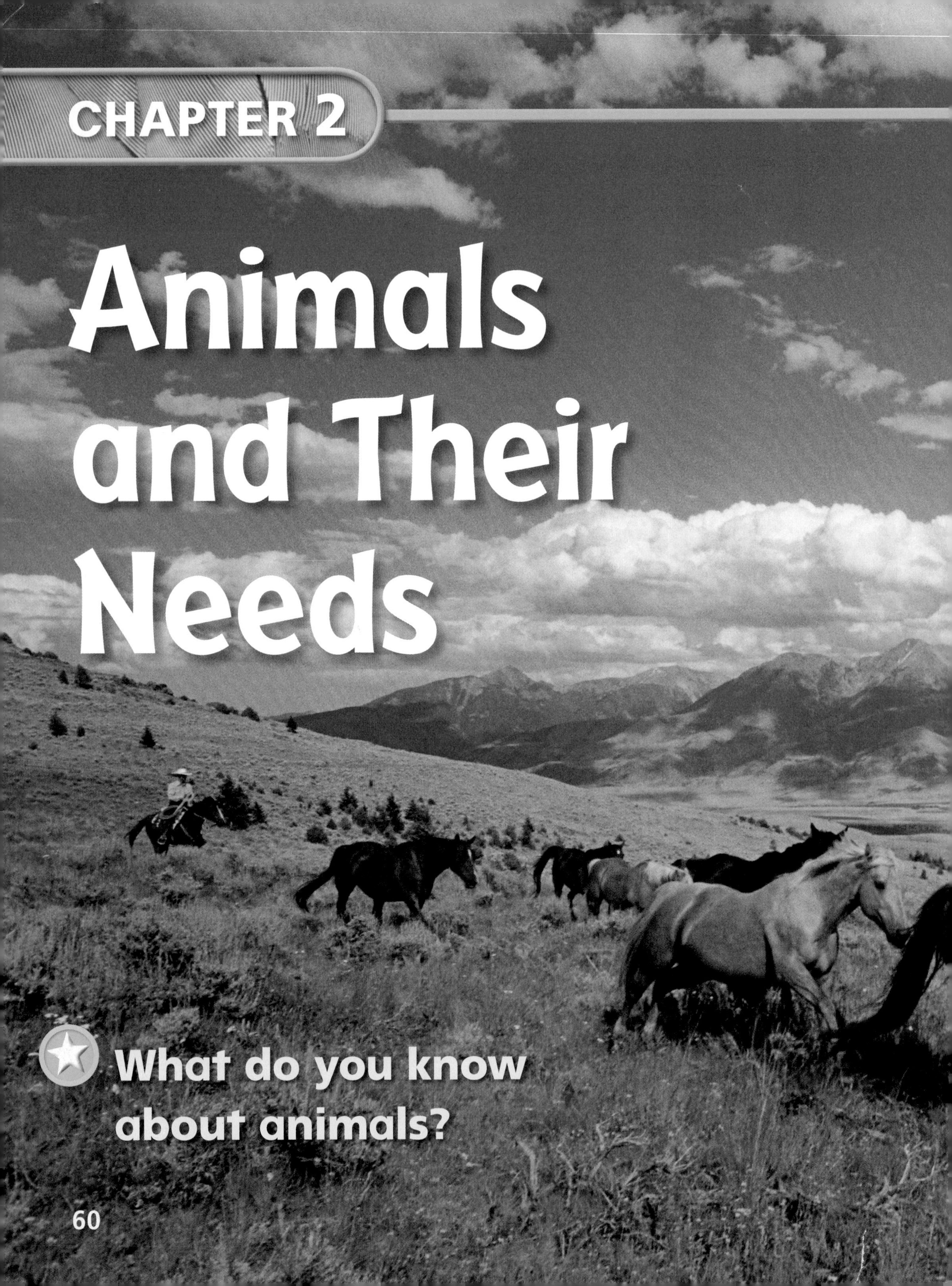

⭐ **What do you know about animals?**

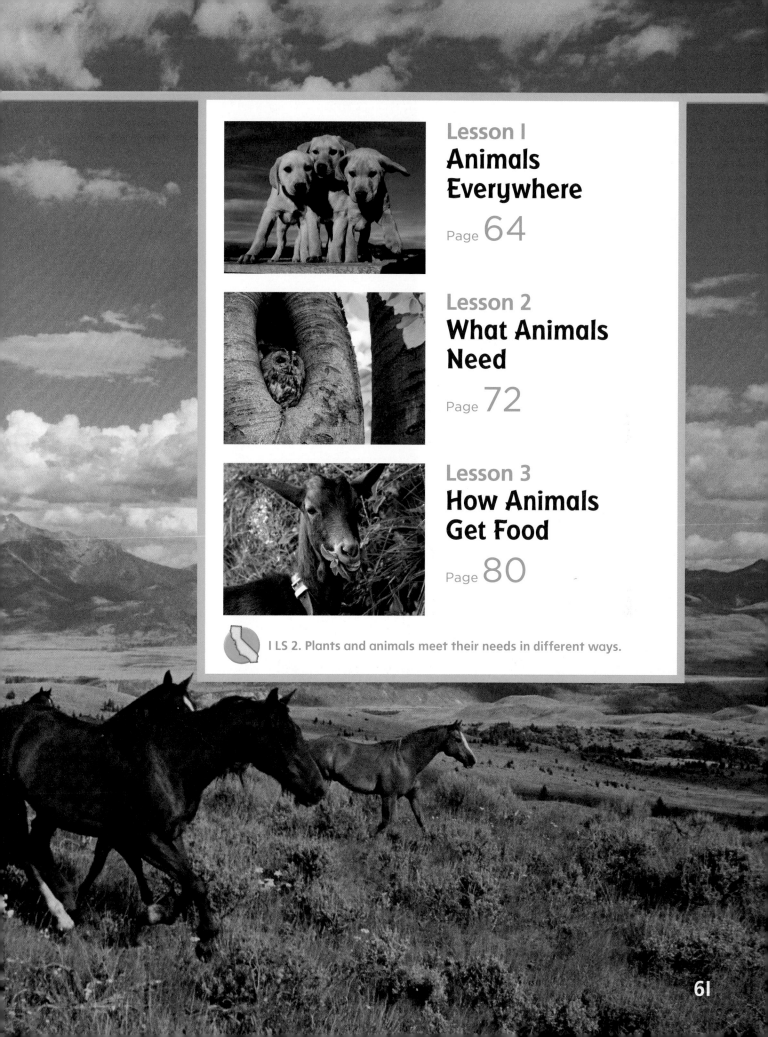

1 LS 2. Plants and animals meet their needs in different ways.

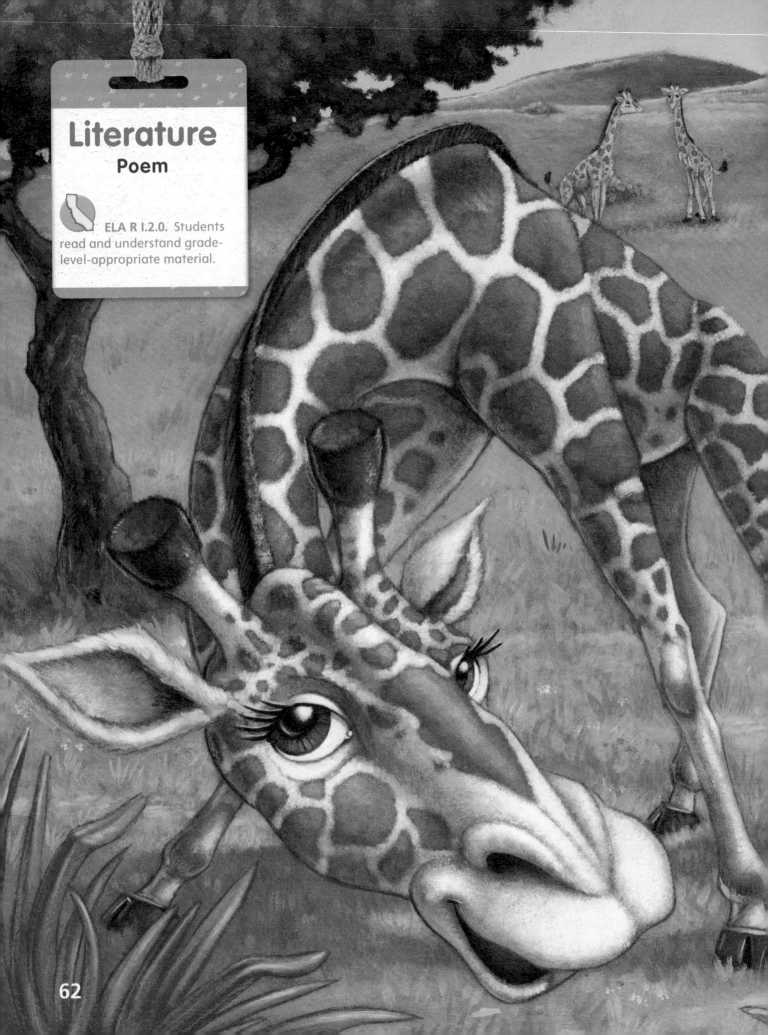

Literature
Poem

Giraffes

by Mary Ann Hoberman

Giraffes
    I like them.
    Ask me why.
        Because they hold their heads up high.
        Because their necks stretch to the sky.
        Because they're quiet, calm, and shy.
        Because they run so fast they fly.
        Because their eyes are velvet brown.
        Because their coats are spotted tan.
        Because they eat the tops of trees.
        Because their legs have knobby knees.
        Because
        Because
        Because. That's why
    I like giraffes.

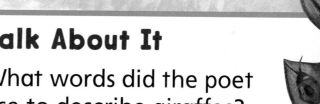

Talk About It

What words did the poet
use to describe giraffes?

Animals Everywhere

Look and Wonder

Are all animals like these animals? Why or why not?

Building block lesson for 1 LS 2.a. Students know different plants and animals inhabit different kinds of environments and have external features that help them thrive in different kinds of places.

What are some different kinds of animals?

What to Do

You need

magazines

scissors

① Cut out pictures of different animals.

② **Classify.** Sort the pictures into groups.

Explore More

③ **Compare.** Are your groups the same as your classmates'? What other animals could you put in each group?

 I IE 4.e. Make new observations when discrepancies exist between two descriptions of the same object or phenomenon.

Vocabulary

mammals
birds
reptiles
insects

What are some types of animals?

There are many different kinds of animals. They come in all shapes and sizes. Animals have different body coverings to help them live in their habitats.

▼ Sea otters' fur keeps them warm and dry in cold water.

▼ Walruses have blubber under their thick skin to help keep them warm.

Mammals are a group of animals with hair or fur. **Birds** are a group of animals that have feathers. Mammals and birds take care of their young. They live in habitats that help their young survive.

✓ Can you name some mammals and birds?

▼ Giraffes are mammals. Mammals give birth to their young.

▲ Ducks are birds. Birds lay eggs.

What are some other types of animals?

Reptiles are a group of animals that have dry skin covered with scales. Snakes, lizards, and alligators are all reptiles. Reptiles lay eggs. Most reptiles do not take care of their young.

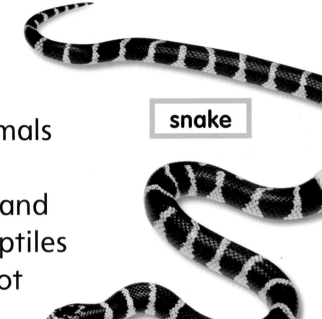
snake

lizard

alligator

Insects are animals that have three body parts and six legs. Ants and butterflies are both insects. Spiders are not insects. They have eight legs.

 Why are spiders not insects?

spider

Ant

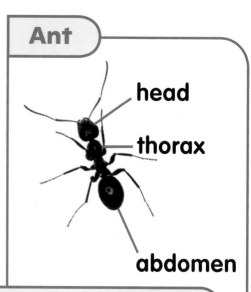

head

thorax

abdomen

Read a Diagram

How do you know this ant is an insect?

Think, Talk, and Write

1. **Compare and Contrast.** How are reptiles like mammals? How are they different?

2. Write about and draw your favorite animal.

Art Link

Make a collage using pictures of reptiles, insects, and mammals.

butterfly

Focus on Skills

Compare

When you **compare** two things, you look for ways that they are the same and different.

Learn It

Ray compared a dog to a turtle. He made a Venn diagram to show how they are the same and different.

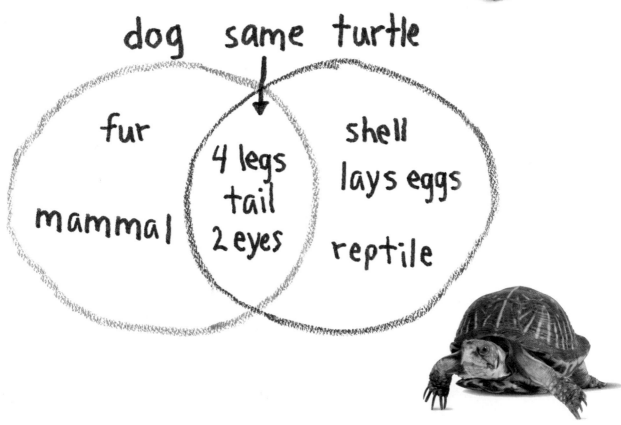

dog   same   turtle

fur

mammal

4 legs
tail
2 eyes

shell
lays eggs

reptile

I IE 4.b. Record observations and data with pictures, numbers, or written statements.

Try It

Look at the pictures of the
alligator and duck.

alligator

duck

I. How are they the same?

2. How are they different?

3. Record what is the same and
different in a Venn diagram.

What Animals Need

Look and Wonder

How is this owl meeting its needs?

 I LS 2.b. Students know both plants and animals need water, animals need food, and plants need light.

What do worms need?

What to Do

1. Collect worms.

2. Place worms, soil, and leaves into your worm habitat.

3. **Observe.** What do you notice about the worms? What do they need?

4. **Record Data.** Draw what you observe.

Explore More

5. **Compare.** How is your worm habitat different from the worm's natural habitat? How is it the same?

 I IE 4.b. Record observations and data with pictures, numbers, or written statements.

You need

worms

clear container

soil

Step 2

Vocabulary

shelter

gills

fins

 SCIENCE QUEST Explore what animals need with the Junior Rangers.

What do animals need to live?

Have you ever taken care of an animal? What did your animal need to live? Animals are living things. They need food, water, and air.

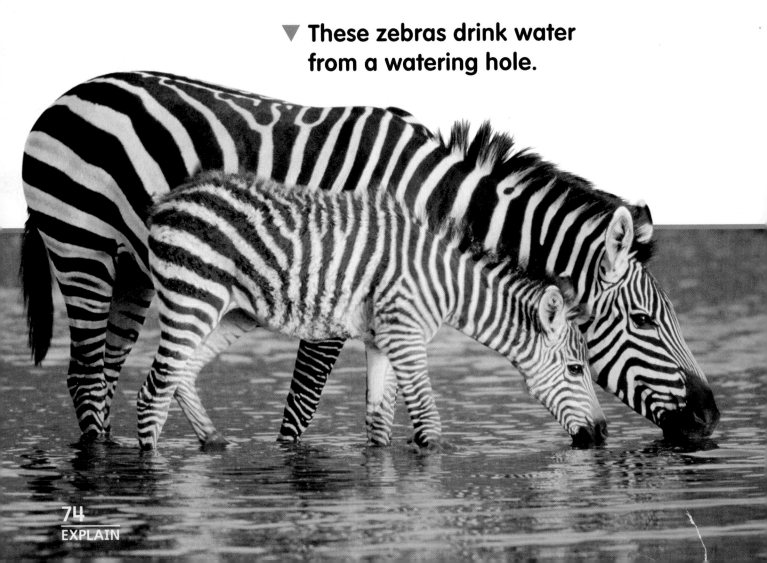

▼ **These zebras drink water from a watering hole.**

Animals live in different kinds of places. Some animals use trees or other plants for shelter. A **shelter** is a place where an animal can be safe.

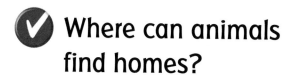 Where can animals find homes?

▲ **These raccoons find shelter in a log.**

▲ **This bear eats a plant for food.**

How do animals' body parts help them survive?

All animals need air to survive. Animals have body parts that help them get air. **Gills** help fish take in air from the water. **Fins** help fish swim in the water.

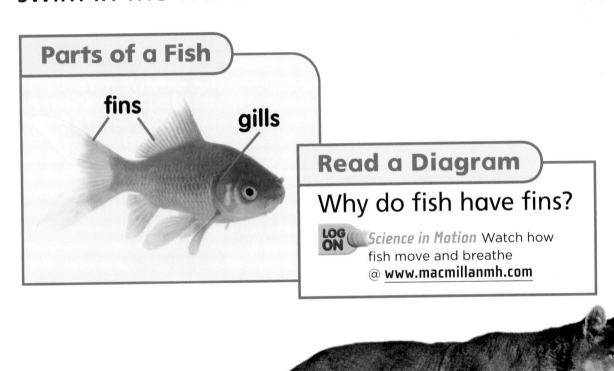

Parts of a Fish

fins

gills

Read a Diagram

Why do fish have fins?

LOG ON *Science in Motion* Watch how fish move and breathe @ **www.macmillanmh.com**

▶ **This mountain lion's legs help it move fast to catch food.**

Animals move to find food and water. Energy gives animals the power to do things. Animals get their energy from the food they eat.

▲ Wings help birds fly to find food.

✓ How do animals use their body parts to get what they need to live?

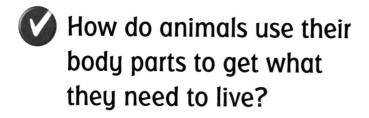

Think, Talk, and Write

1. **Compare and Contrast.** How do fish and birds meet their needs?

2. Write about how you would help an animal meet its needs.

Health Link

How do you meet your needs?

LOG ON e-Review Summaries and quizzes online @ www.macmillanmh.com

Animals' Needs

Look at the picture below. How is this girl making sure her cat gets what it needs?

 Write a Story

Write about how this girl cares for her cat. Tell what she does first, next, and last.

Remember

Tell what happens first, next, and last.

 e-Journal Write about it online @ www.macmillanmh.com

 ELA W I.2.2. Write brief expository descriptions of a real object, person, place, or event, using sensory details.

Animal Graph

Tom made a bar graph to show what kinds of pets his friends have at home.

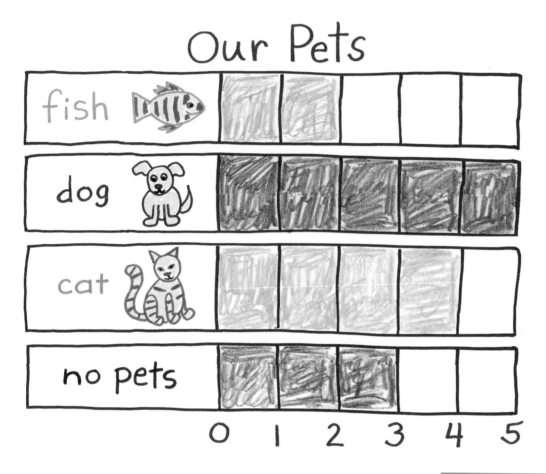

Our Pets

fish
dog
cat
no pets

0 1 2 3 4 5

Make a Graph

Ask your classmates which is their favorite pet. Make a bar graph to show what you find out.

Remember

A bar graph helps to answer questions.

 MA SDAP I.I.2. Represent and compare data (e.g., largest, smallest, most often, least often) by using pictures, bar graphs, tally charts, and picture graphs.

How Animals Get Food

Look and Wonder

What kinds of food does this animal eat?

 I LS 2.d. Students know how to infer what animals eat from the shape of their teeth (e.g., sharp teeth: eats meat; flat teeth: eats plants).

How do teeth help you eat different foods?

1. **Observe.** Try each type of food. Use a mirror to see which teeth you use.

2. **Record Data.** Draw and write about which teeth you used.

3. **Compare.** Look at the shape of your teeth. Why are they different?

Explore More

4. **Predict.** Which teeth would you use to chew a piece of meat? Why?

You need

carrots

dried fruit

popcorn

mirror

 1 IE 4.b. Record observations and data with pictures, numbers, or written statements.

Step 1

Vocabulary

herbivore

carnivore

What animals eat plants?

Animals eat food to get the energy they need to live. Different animals eat different things. Some animals are herbivores. A **herbivore** is an animal that only eats plants.

horse

Horses and rabbits are herbivores. Can you think of other animals that eat only plants?

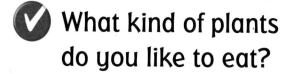 What kind of plants do you like to eat?

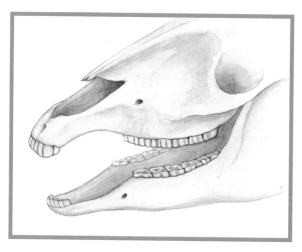

▲ **Herbivores have flat teeth to chew and grind plants.**

rabbit

What animals eat meat?

Some animals are carnivores. A **carnivore** is an animal that eats only other animals. Tigers and sharks are both carnivores. Can you think of other animals that eat only animals?

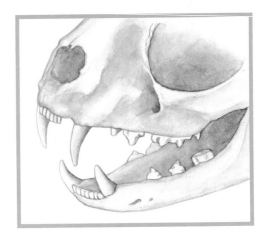

▲ Carnivores have sharp teeth to rip and tear meat.

shark

tiger

Animal Teeth	
Carnivore	**Herbivore**
sharp teeth	flat teeth
rip and tear meat	chew and grind plants
tigers and sharks	horses and rabbits

✔ If an animal eats both plants and animals, what kind of teeth might it have?

Read a Chart

Why do tigers and horses have different kinds of teeth?

Think, Talk, and Write

1. **Compare and Contrast.** How are your teeth like a carnivore's?

2. Write about and draw an animal that eats only plants.

Health Link

Why do you have to take care of your teeth?

Be a Scientist

animal cards

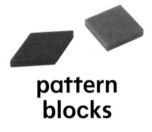

clay

pattern blocks

What do animals eat?

Find out what kinds of food different animals eat.

What to Do

① **Compare.** Look at the pictures. How are the animals alike? How are they different?

cow

Macmillian/McGraw-Hill
Photograph by Brand X Pictures/Getty Images   17

tiger

Macmillian/McGraw-Hill
Photograph by Brand X Pictures/Getty Images   18

② **Infer.** What kinds of food does the animal in each picture eat? How do you know?

 I LS 2.d. Students know how to infer what animals eat from the shape of their teeth (e.g., sharp teeth: eats meat; flat teeth: eats plants).

3 **Make a Model.** Use clay to make a model of a carnivore's and a herbivore's teeth.

Step **3**

4 **Communicate.** Explain to a classmate what type of teeth each animal has.

Investigate More

Observe. Visit a pet store or nature center. How do the animals eat their food?

Meet Jin Meng

Some animals like Tyrannosaurus rex lived long ago. How do we know what these animals ate? Scientists like Jin Meng study fossils. Fossils are what is left of living things from the past.

Jin works at the American Museum of Natural History. He looks closely at the fossil's teeth. They are long and sharp. Jin thinks the animal was a carnivore.

When Jin looks at the animal's stomach, he finds the bones of a small dinosaur. It was definitely a meat eater!

▶ **Small dinosaur bones found inside the stomach of this animal fossil tell us the dinosaur ate meat.**

ELA R I.2.0. Students read and understand grade-level-appropriate material.

Talk About It

Compare and Contrast. How are a dinosaur's teeth different from yours?

LOG ON e-Journal Write about it online @ **www.macmillanmh.com**

▲ **Jin Meng**

◀ **Scientists put bones together to help us learn what dinosaurs looked liked.**

AMERICAN MUSEUM OF NATURAL HISTORY

My Animal Book

Big ones, little ones,
and fat ones, too.
Have you seen animals
at the zoo?

Do you like insects?
They live in many places.
Do you like bats?
They live in dark spaces.

Do you like snakes?

They have scales.

Do you like birds?

They have feathers for tails.

Do you like horses?

They like to run.

Do you like lizards?

They lie in the Sun.

All animals need to eat.

Some like plants.

Some like meat.

Do you have a pet that
needs your care?
All animals need food,
water, and air.

Vocabulary

bird, page 67

mammals, page 67

reptile, page 68

shelter, page 75

carnivore, page 84

What does each picture show?

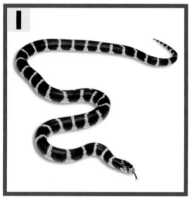

I LS 2.a

I LS 2.a

I LS 2.a

Complete each sentence.

4. A place where an animal can live and be safe is called a _____. I LS 2.b

5. An animal that eats only meat is called a _____. I LS 2.d

6. Why do animals move? I LS 2.b

7. Compare. Use a Venn diagram to compare the animals in the pictures below. I LS 2.d

Venn diagram

8. Compare and Contrast. Write how insects and birds are the same and different. I LS 2.a

 What do you know about animals? I LS 2

What Do They Need?

carnivore

herbivore

▶ How do each of these animals get what they need?

▶ Write about what each animal eats.

▶ Draw pictures to show what each animal's teeth look like.

I LS 2.d. Students know how to infer what animals eat from the shape of their teeth (e.g., sharp teeth: eats meat; flat teeth: eats plants).

1 **Which animal is a carnivore?** I LS 2.d

A horse

B tiger

C rabbit

D cow

2 **The drawing shows an insect.**

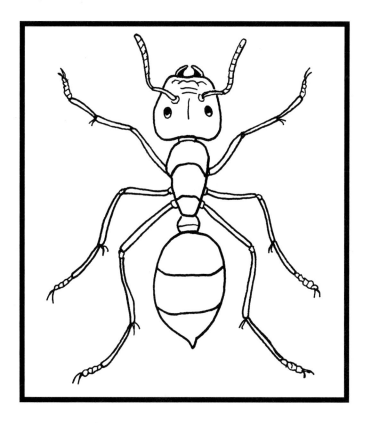

How many legs do insects have? I LS 2.a

A 2

B 4

C 5

D 6

Plants and Animals Together

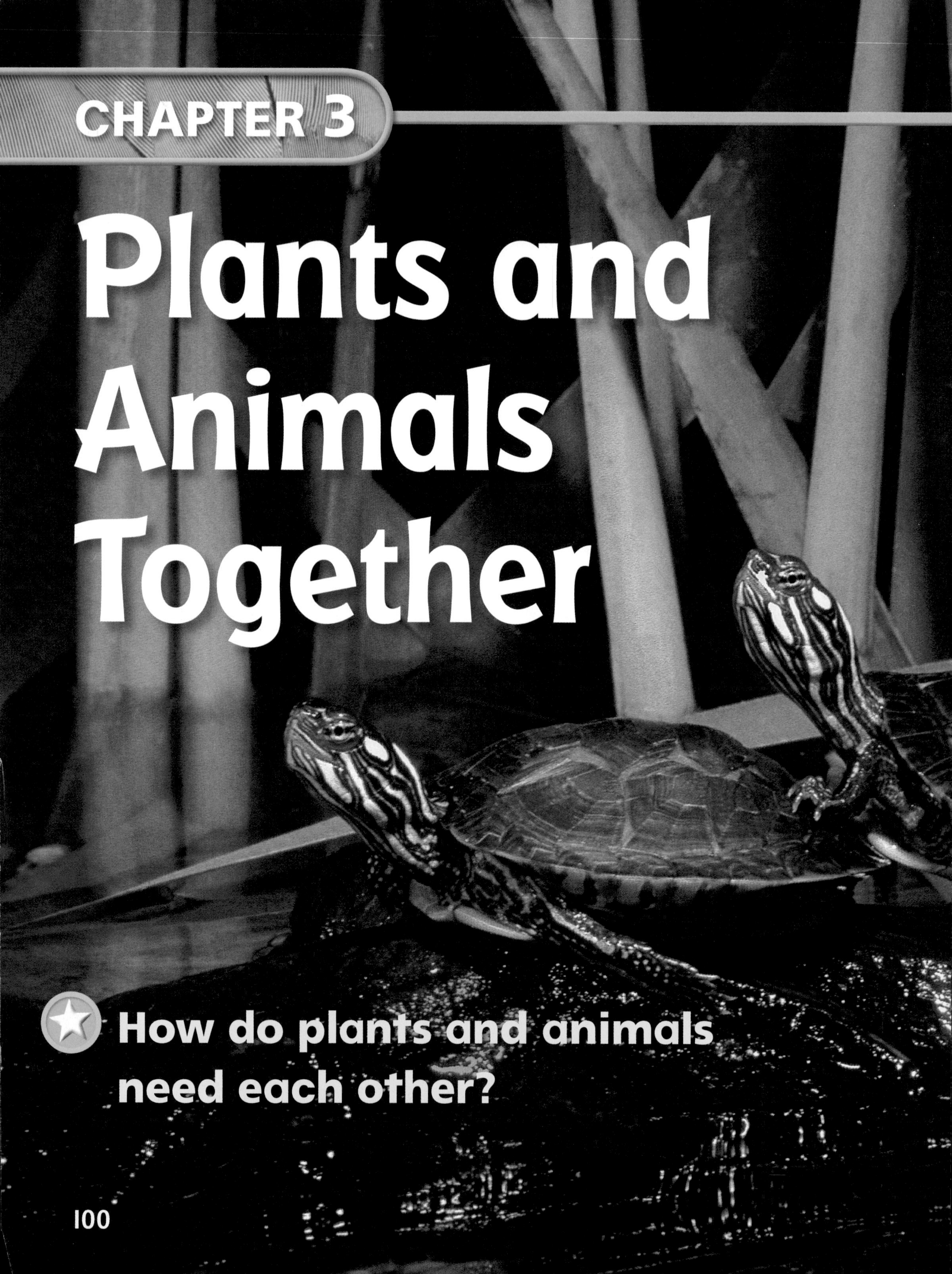

⭐ How do plants and animals need each other?

 1 LS 2. Plants and animals meet their needs in different ways.

Literature

Poem

ELA R 1.2.0. Students read and understand grade-level-appropriate material.

To Be a Clover

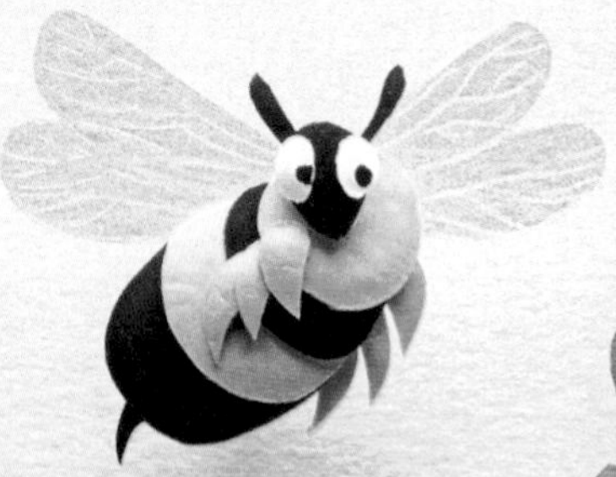

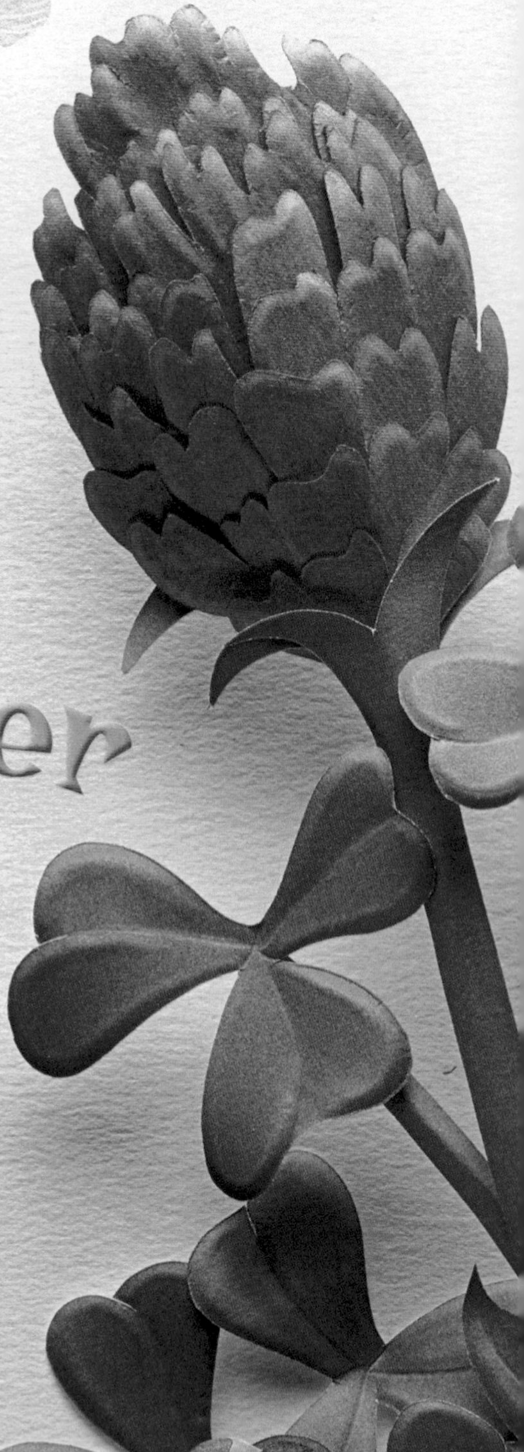

by Aileen Fisher

I wonder how it would feel
to be a clover
with a bee buzzing over
and landing in my hair
on three pair of tickly feet,
looking for something to eat?

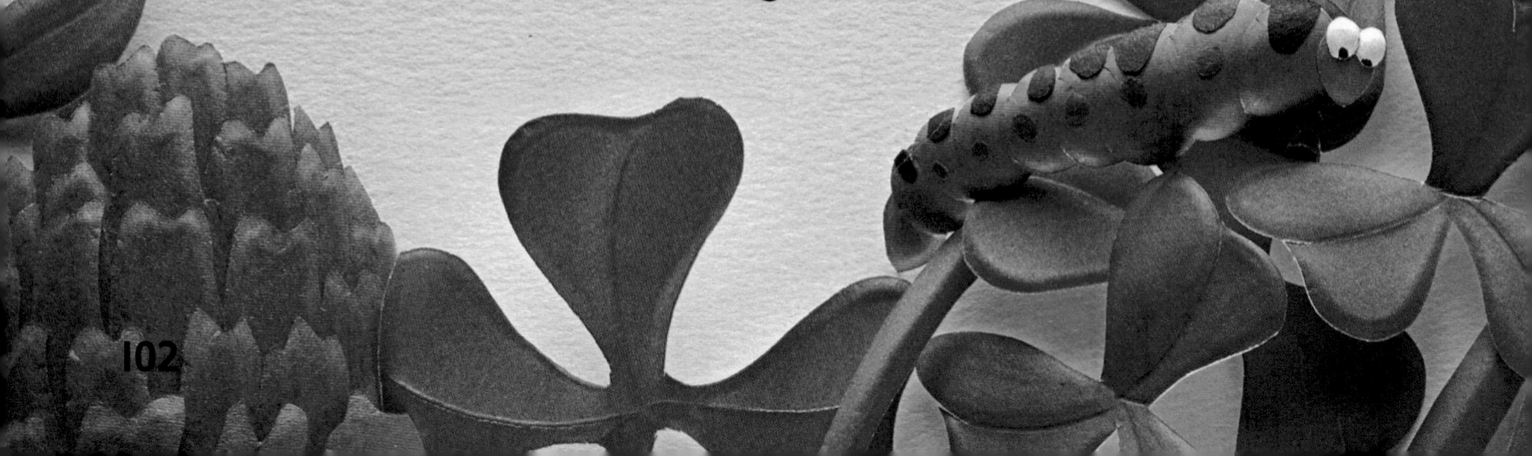

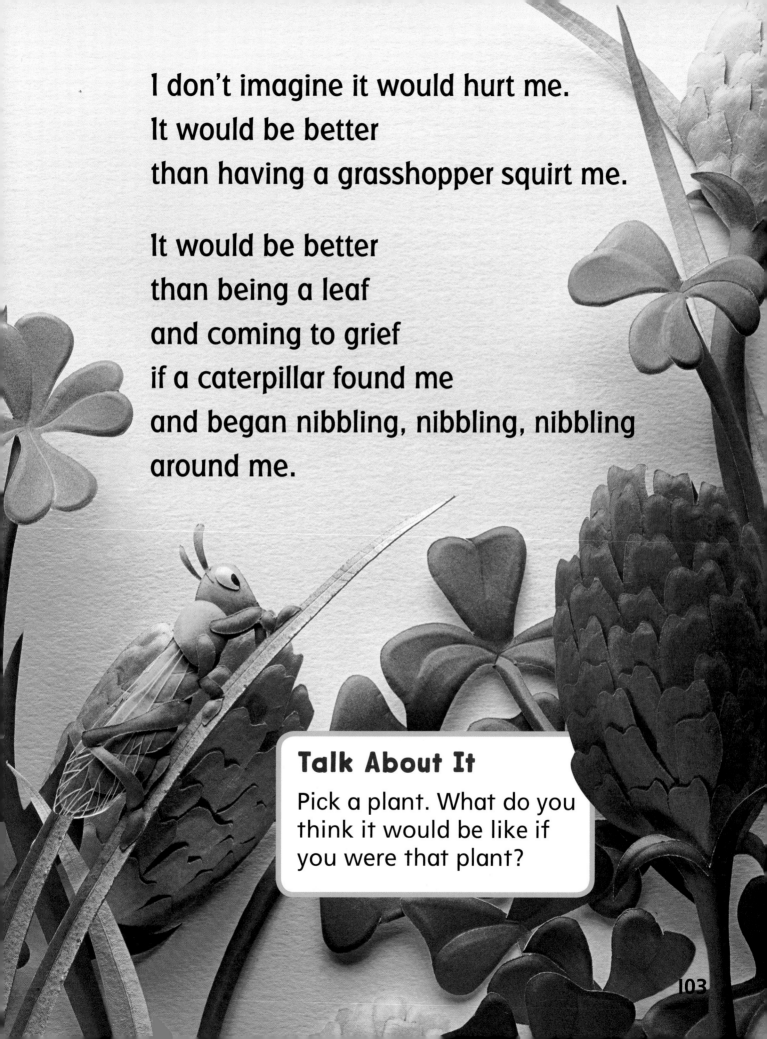

I don't imagine it would hurt me.
It would be better
than having a grasshopper squirt me.

It would be better
than being a leaf
and coming to grief
if a caterpillar found me
and began nibbling, nibbling, nibbling
around me.

Talk About It

Pick a plant. What do you think it would be like if you were that plant?

Land Habitats

Joshua Tree National Park, California

Look and Wonder

What kinds of plants and animals live in the desert?

 I LS 2.a. Students know different plants and animals inhabit different kinds of environments and have external features that help them thrive in different kinds of places.

What kinds of plants and animals live together?

What to Do

1. Draw an animal. Draw the plants that live with the animal.

2. **Communicate.** Share your picture with a partner. Tell how plants and animals get what they need to live.

Explore More

3. **Infer.** Why do plants and animals live together?

I IE 4.a. Draw pictures that portray some features of the thing being described.

You need

paper

crayons

Step 1

Vocabulary

grassland

adaptation

forest

 SCIENCE QUEST Explore plants and animals with the Junior Rangers.

How do plants and animals live in a grassland?

Many animals live in grasslands. A **grassland** is a dry place with a lot of grass. Some of the animals that live in a grassland are small. They can hide from animals that might eat them.

▲ Prairie dogs hide in holes in the ground. Their color helps them blend in.

Other animals are too big to hide. They have to stay safe in other ways. An **adaptation** is a special feature that helps an animal stay alive in its habitat.

✓ How is a giraffe's long neck an adaptation?

▶ Giraffes have long necks that help them to spot animals that might eat them and to eat the leaves off tall trees.

How do plants and animals live in a forest?

A tree can be a home for many animals and even for plants. A **forest** is a place where there are a lot of trees. Some trees grow tall in the forest. This helps them get the sunlight they need to make food.

moose in forest

Some animals use the trees for food. Other animals eat nuts and insects found on the trees.

✔ Why is a forest a good place for plants and animals to live?

Read a Photo

How is this plant helping the woodpecker meet its needs?

Think, Talk, and Write

1. **Classify and Categorize.** Which animals live in a grassland? Why?

2. Write words to describe a forest.

Art Link

Draw an animal that lives in a grassland.

Communicate

When you **communicate** you write, draw, or tell your ideas.

Roger looked at a picture of the desert. He wrote what he saw in a web.

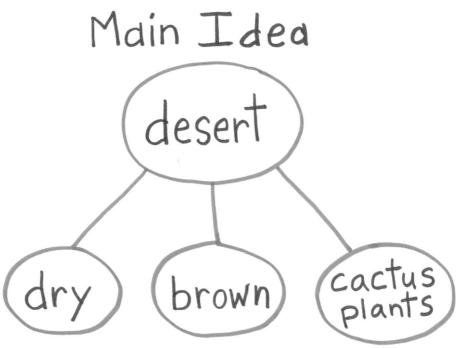

Main Idea

desert

dry   brown   cactus plants

 I IE 4.b. Record observations and data with pictures, numbers, or written statements.

Try It

Look at the picture below.

Mojave yucca, Joshua Tree National Park

1. What shape are the leaves?
What color are they?

2. What does the ground look
like?

3. Communicate by filling in your
own web about the picture.

Water Habitats

Look and Wonder

Earth is covered with more water than land. What plants and animals live in water?

 Building block lesson for I LS 2.c. Students know animals eat plants or other animals for food and may also use plants or even other animals for shelter and nesting.

How do plants and animals live in water?

You need

clear tank

pebbles

water plant

fish

What to Do

1. **Make a Model.** Put pebbles, a plant, water, and a fish in a tank.

2. **Observe.** How does the fish move in water?

3. **Communicate.** Draw a picture of your aquarium.

Explore More

4. **Infer.** How does the plant help the fish live in water?

 1 IE 4.b. Record observations and data with pictures, numbers, or written statements.

Step 1

Vocabulary

pond

ocean

What lives in a pond?

Have you ever been to a pond? What animals and plants did you see? A **pond** is a small body of fresh water. Fresh water has little or no salt in it.

Pond Habitat

Read a Photo

What living things do you see at this pond?

Plants and animals live together in ponds. They need each other to survive. Many animals find food and shelter in a pond.

✓ How do plants help animals live in a pond?

beaver

▲ Beavers use trees to build dams so they have a safe place to live.

What helps plants and animals live in the ocean?

Have you ever gone swimming in the ocean? An **ocean** is salty water that is very large and deep.

orca whale

There are many different mammals, fish, and plants that live in the ocean. They need each other to survive in the ocean.

✓ What plants and animals do you know live in the ocean?

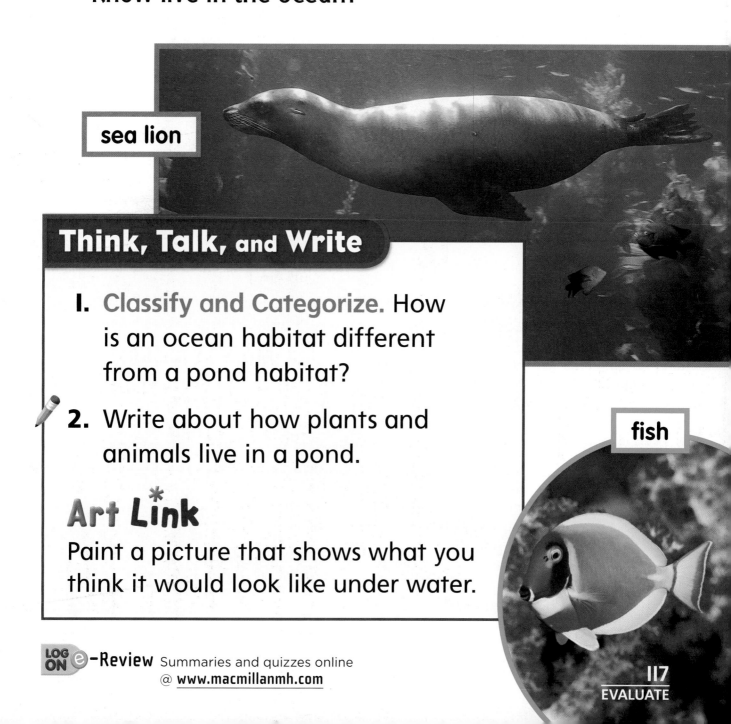

sea lion

Think, Talk, and Write

1. **Classify and Categorize.** How is an ocean habitat different from a pond habitat?

2. Write about how plants and animals live in a pond.

Art Link

Paint a picture that shows what you think it would look like under water.

fish

Meet Mark Siddall

Most people stay away from leeches. Mark Siddall goes looking for them!

Mark is a scientist at the American Museum of Natural History. He finds leeches in the ocean, swamps, ponds, and streams.

Mark wants to know how many different leeches there are and how they take care of their young.

▲ **Mark in his lab**

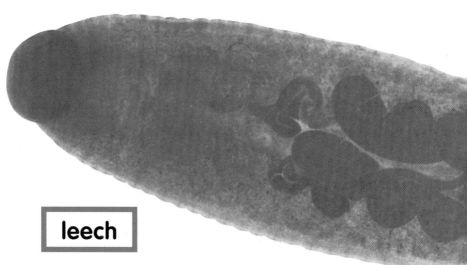

leech

ELA R 1.2.0. Students read and understand grade-level-appropriate material.

▶ Mark is an invertebrate zoologist. That's a scientist who studies animals without backbones.

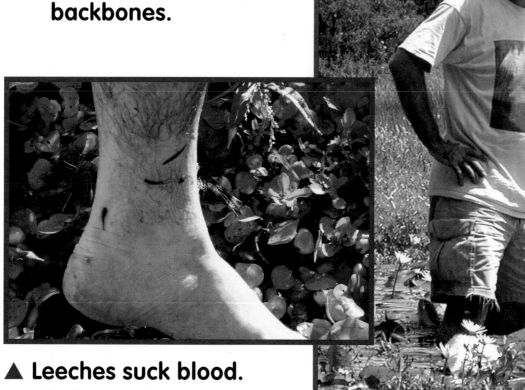

▲ Leeches suck blood. Mark uses his ankles as bait.

Talk About It

Classify and Categorize. What other living things can live in water?

LOG ON ℮-Journal Write about it online @ **www.macmillanmh.com**

AMERICAN MUSEUM OF NATURAL HISTORY

Plants and Animals Need Each Other

Look and Wonder

Animals and plants need each other to survive. How do these plants and animals help each other?

 1 LS 2.c. Students know animals eat plants or other animals for food and may also use plants or even other animals for shelter and nesting.

Why do plants and animals live together?

What to Do

1. **Observe.** Look closely at a plant near your school.

2. **Classify.** What animals can you find near, in, or on the plant?

3. **Record Data.** Draw a picture of what you observed.

Explore More

4. **Communicate.** How is the plant helping the animals survive?

 I IE 4.b. Record observations and data with pictures, numbers, or written statements.

You need

paper

crayons

Step **1**

Vocabulary

pollen

How do plants and animals help each other?

Plants help animals live. Animals use plants for shelter and food.

◀ **This field mouse eats berries from a plant.**

▲ **These skunks use a plant as their home.**

Animals help plants live, too. Bees help plants make new plants. Bees carry pollen from flower to flower. **Pollen** is powder inside a flower that makes seeds.

✔ How do plants and animals need each other?

▲ **Pollen sticks to the bee's legs.**

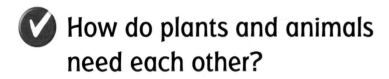
Spider Web

Read a Photo

How does the spider use the plants?

Why do some animals need other animals?

Animals need each other to survive. Sometimes animals can be helpful to one another. Insects that live on a zebra can be harmful. But a bird can eat the insects. Birds can also warn a zebra of danger.

▼ **This bird eats insects that might live on the zebra.**

▼ Fleas are harmful to dogs.

Other times, one animal is helped and the other animal is harmed. When a flea lives on a dog, it feeds off the dog and can make the dog sick.

✔ Why do animals need other animals?

Think, Talk, and Write

1. **Classify and Categorize.** What are some animals that need other animals to live?

2. Write about how an animal uses plants to live.

Health Link

Draw and write about how plants help you stay healthy.

You need

peanut butter

paper roll

craft stick

bird seeds

string

paper plate

How do animals need plants to survive?

Find out how birds need plants.

What to Do

1 Spread peanut butter onto a paper roll with a craft stick.

Step 1

2 Cover the roll completely with bird seeds. Wash your hands.

Step 2

 I IE 4.b. Record observations and data with pictures, numbers, or written statements.

3. Loop a piece of string through the paper roll. Tie both ends of the string in a knot. Hang the bird feeder on a tree branch outside.

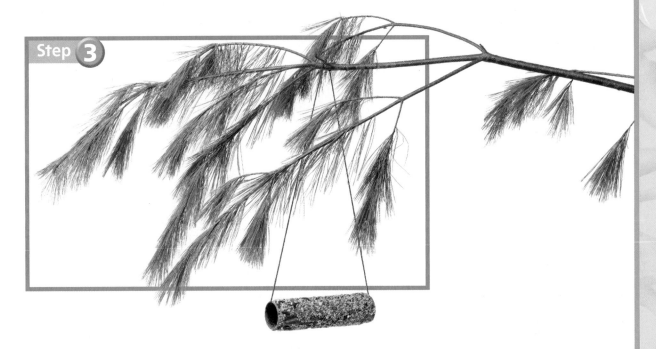

Step 3

4. **Observe.** Look at the bird feeder every day for one week.

5. **Record Data.** Draw the different kinds of birds that you see.

Investigate More

Communicate. How do the birds use plant seeds to survive?

Food Chains

Look and Wonder

What kinds of animals live around you? What do they eat? Where do they get their food?

I LS 2.c. Students know animals eat plants or other animals for food and may also use plants or even other animals for shelter and nesting.

What do animals eat?

You need

paper

crayons

What to Do

① Communicate. Draw a picture of a plant. Draw a picture of an animal that eats that plant. Draw a picture of an animal that eats that animal.

② Put Things in Order. Put your drawings in order to show what happens to the plant and animals.

③ Classify. What animals eat plants? What animals eat other animals?

Step **①**

Explore More

④ Infer. What kinds of food do people eat?

 I IE 4.a. Draw pictures that portray some features of the thing being described.

Vocabulary

food chain
omnivore

What is a food chain?

All living things need food. Food gives them energy. A **food chain** shows the order in which living things get the food they need.

Food Chain

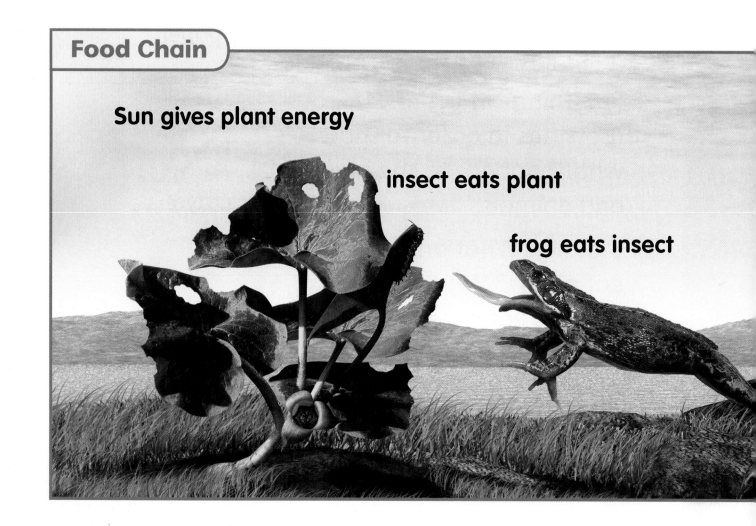

Sun gives plant energy

insect eats plant

frog eats insect

Herbivores eat plants. Carnivores eat animals. An **omnivore** eats both plants and animals.

✓ What kinds of food do you eat?

owl eats frog

Read a Diagram

What is the first living thing in this food chain?

LOG ON *Science in Motion* Watch a food chain @ **www.macmillanmh.com**

What happens in a food chain?

The Sun is the beginning of every food chain. Without the Sun, plants could not grow and there would be no food for animals.

▼ **This shows a water food chain.**

Tuna eats anchovies.

Anchovies eat small animals.

Small animals eat plants.

Plants are the first link in most food chains. People are at the top of many food chains.

✔ **What would happen if there were no fish?**

People fish for tuna to eat.

Think, Talk, and Write

1. **Classify and Categorize.** What animals eat only plants?

2. Write about the food chain that ended with your breakfast.

Health Link

Act out a story about a food chain.

Animal Facts

Some animals eat other animals. The arctic fox eats lemmings and other small animals.

 Write About It

Write about how the arctic fox gets what it needs to survive.

Remember
Give information about one main idea.

 e-Journal Write about it online @ **www.macmillanmh.com**

 ELA W I.2.2. Write brief expository descriptions of a real object, person, place, or event, using sensory details.

Number Story

Donna drank one glass of juice. Donna's little brother also drank one glass of juice.

Donna's older sister drank two glasses of juice.

How many glasses of juice did Donna's family drink?

Write Your Own Story

Make up a story to tell how many tacos Donna's family ate for dinner.

How many tacos did the family eat?
How many tacos had cheese?

Remember

A number sentence helps to solve a problem.

MA AF 1.1. Write and solve number sentences from problem situations that express relationships involving addition and subtraction.

135
EXTEND

Plants and Animals

There are lots of places
you can go
to see where plants
and animals grow.

You can go to a forest to
see a woodpecker peck.

You can go to a grassland
to see a giraffe's long neck.

Some animals live in salt water,
like fish and the furry sea otter.

Some animals live in lakes,
like ducks and scaly snakes.

Do plants need animals?

Yes, they do.

Animals need plants.
So do you!

Vocabulary

adaptation, page 107

food chain, page 130

forest, page 108

ocean, page 116

Complete each sentence.

1. A habitat with many trees is called a _____. I LS 2.a

2. The picture below is a _____. I LS 2.c

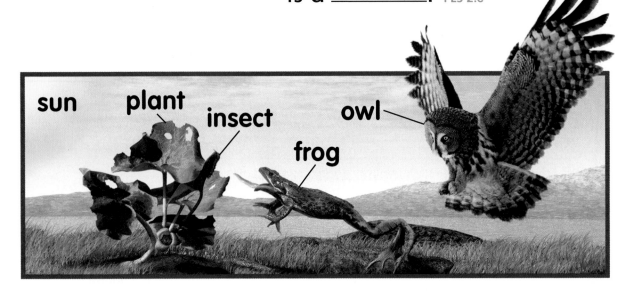

sun   plant   insect   frog   owl

3. Giraffes have long necks to help them eat the leaves off tall trees. This is called an _____. I LS 2.a

4. Salty water that is very large and deep is called an _____. I LS 2.a

5. What helps prairie dogs live in grasslands? I LS 2.a

6. Communicate. Describe a food chain. I LS 2.c

7. Classify and Categorize. Describe a land and water habitat. I LS 2.a

 How do plants and animals need each other? I LS 2

CHAPTER 3

Animal Habitats

Animals live in different habitats.

▶ Choose one animal. Draw the plants and animals that live in its habitat.

▶ Describe the animal's habitat.

▶ Explain how it gets what it needs to survive.

▶ How do the plants and animals help each other survive in the habitat?

I LS 2.a. Students know different plants and animals inhabit different kinds of environments and have external features that help them thrive in different kinds of places.

1 **The first living thing in a food chain is always** _____. I LS 2.c

   A an animal

   B a plant

   C a carnivore

   D the Sun

2 **Sea otters live in the ocean.**

The sea otter's _____ **helps it survive in the cold water.** I LS 2.a

   A fur

   B color

   C feathers

   D teeth

Insect-Eating PLANTS

Plants make food from energy they get from the Sun. Did you know that some plants also eat animals?

Venus's-flytrap

▼ **A grasshopper lands on the leaf.**

▼ **The leaf snaps closed.**

Trapped! Long spines hold the grasshopper inside. Juices from the plant digest the insect.

Pitcher plant

Splash! Flies fall into the cup-shaped leaf. They can not crawl out. The plant eats the insects.

▲ **flies trapped in a Pitcher plant**

Sundew

A mosquito sees sweet drops on a leaf. Oh no! The drops are sticky. The mosquito is stuck. The leaf slowly closes and the insect is lunch.

▲ **mosquito stuck on a Sundew**

 I LS 2.b. Students know both plants and animals need water, animals need food, and plants need light.
ELA R I.2.0. Students read and understand grade-level-appropriate material.

Veterinarian

Do you love taking care of animals? One day you could become a veterinarian. A veterinarian is a doctor for animals.

Many veterinarians care for pets. They help cats, dogs, birds, and other small animals. They also help cows, horses, and other big farm animals.

Veterinarians need to study science so that they can take care of animals.

veterinarian

More careers for people who love animals.

animal keeper

wildlife manager

Earth Science

The Sun is always behind you when you see a rainbow.

CHAPTER 4

Weather

 What do you know about weather?

I ES 3. Weather can be observed, measured, and described.

Literature
Poem

ELA R I.2.0. Students read and understand grade-level-appropriate material.

Sudden Storm

by Elizabeth Coatsworth

The rain comes in sheets
Sweeping the streets,
Here, here, and here,
Umbrellas appear,

Red, blue, yellow, green,
They tilt and they lean
Like mushrooms, like flowers
That grow when it showers.

Talk About It

How is an umbrella
like a mushroom? How
would you describe rain?

153

Lesson 1

Describe Weather

Look and Wonder

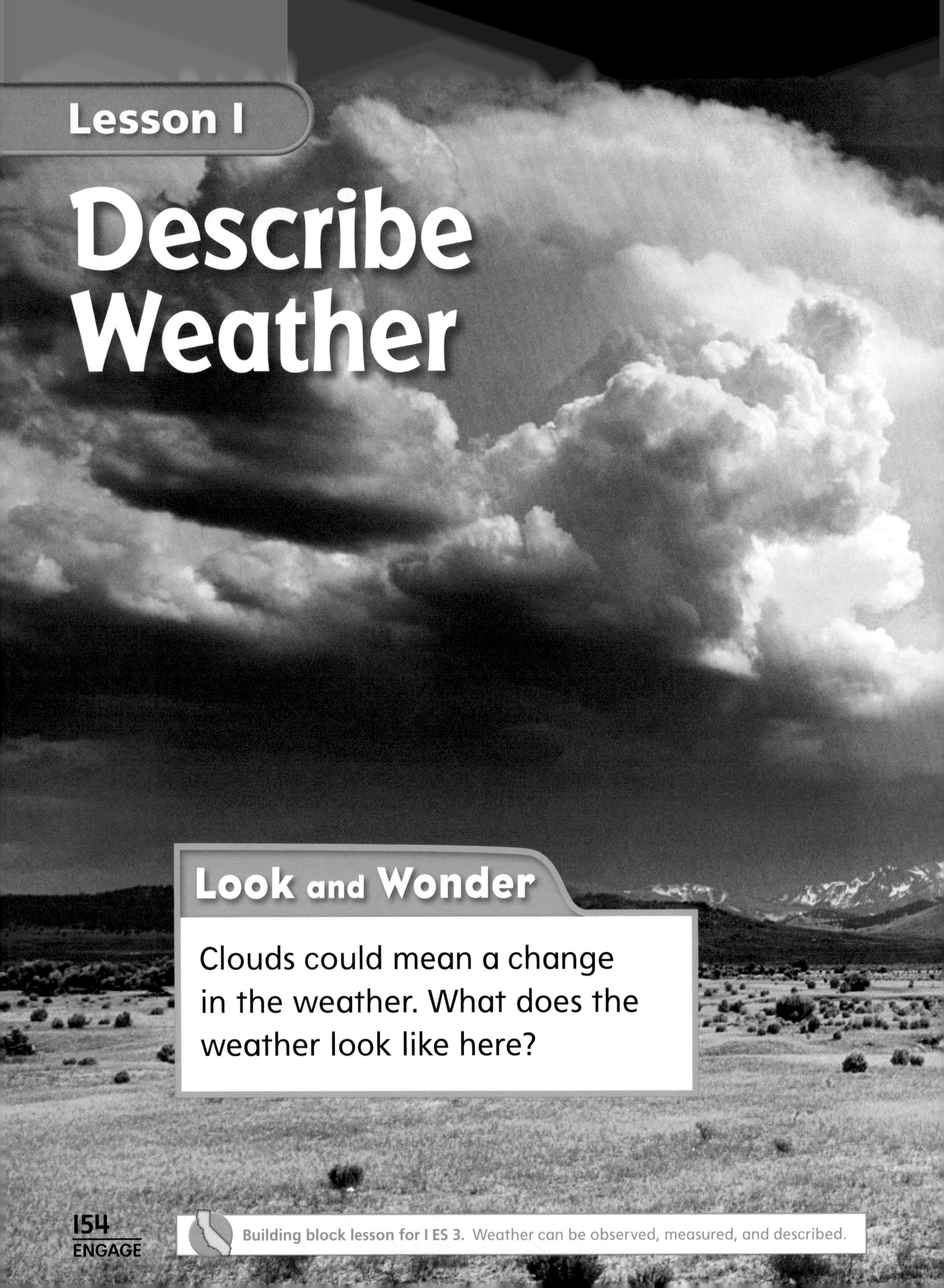

Clouds could mean a change in the weather. What does the weather look like here?

Building block lesson for 1 ES 3. Weather can be observed, measured, and described.

What is today's weather?

What to Do

① **Observe.** Look outside. What is the weather like today?

② **Communicate.** Draw a picture of today's weather.

Explore More

③ **Predict.** What will the weather be like tomorrow?

 I IE 4.a. Draw pictures that portray some features of the thing being described.

You need

paper

crayons

Step **2**

A sunny day with some wind.

Vocabulary

weather
temperature
wind

What is weather?

You probably think about the weather every day. **Weather** is what the air and sky are like each day.

sunny

cloudy

The air might be warm or cool.
The sky might be sunny or cloudy.
The weather might be rainy,
snowy, or dry.

rainy

snowy

 Why is it important to know what
the weather will be?

How can weather change?

Weather changes from day to day.
Temperature is how cold or warm
the air is. Sometimes the air feels
cold. Sometimes the air feels warm.

The sky can change too.
Some days the sky is clear.
Some days the sky is full of clouds.

▲ **This is a cold day.**

▲ **This is a warm day.**

Windy Day

Read a Photo

Which way is the wind blowing?

Wind can change too.
Wind is moving air.
Sometimes wind moves slowly.
Sometimes wind moves very fast.

✔️ How does temperature affect you?

Think, Talk, and Write

1. **Make Predictions.** What will the weather be like tomorrow?

 2. Write words that describe weather.

Art Link

Draw a picture of something you can wear to stay warm on a cold day.

Predict

When you **predict**, you use what you know to tell what will happen.

Learn It

Cindy looked closely at the picture below and made a prediction. You can record your predictions in a chart like the one Cindy made.

What I Predict	What Happens
It will rain and the game will stop.	

 I IE 4.b. Record observations and data with pictures, numbers, or written statements.

Try It

Look at the picture below.

1. What do you know about the weather in the picture?

2. What do you think the children will do?

3. Use a chart like Cindy's to predict what the weather will be like when you go home today. Write what happens.

The Warmth of the Sun

vineyards, Napa Valley, California

Look and Wonder

The Sun makes your skin feel warm. It helps plants grow. What else do you think the Sun does?

I ES 3.c. Students know the sun warms the land, air, and water.

What will the Sun do?

What to Do

1 Fill two cups with soil. Feel the soil in both cups. Put one cup of soil in a sunny place. Put the other cup in a shady place. Wait one hour.

2 **Compare.** Feel the soil in both cups. Draw and write about what happened.

Explore More

3 **Predict.** How might the soil feel at night?

 I IE 4.b. Record observations and data with pictures, numbers, or written statements.

Step **2**

Vocabulary

Sun

water vapor

SCIENCE QUEST Explore the warmth of the Sun with the Junior Rangers.

What does the Sun do?

Have you ever walked on a sandy beach on a hot, sunny day? How did the sand feel? How did the air feel?

The **Sun** is a star. Energy from the Sun heats Earth. The energy of the Sun warms the land, air, and water. It helps to make wind, rain, clouds, and even snow.

✓ When do you feel the heat of the Sun?

Sun

What does the Sun do to water?

As the Sun warms water, some water turns into water vapor. **Water vapor** is water that goes up into the air. You can not see it, but it is there.

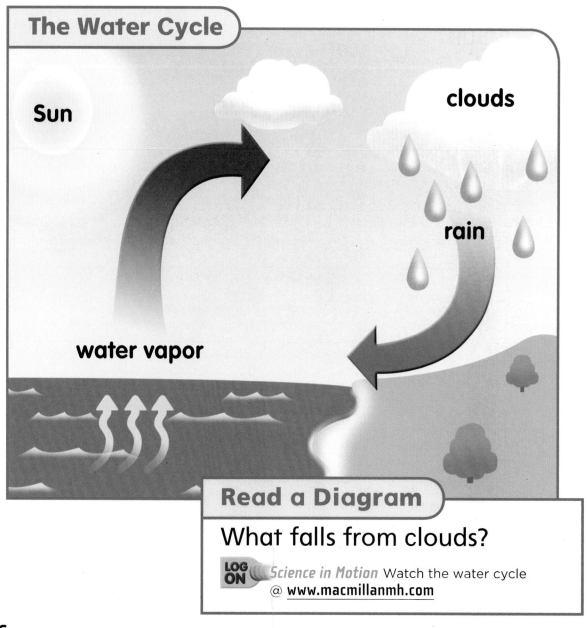

The Water Cycle

Sun

clouds

rain

water vapor

Read a Diagram

What falls from clouds?

LOG ON *Science in Motion* Watch the water cycle @ **www.macmillanmh.com**

As water vapor cools in the sky, it turns back into drops of water or bits of ice. Clouds are made of both. When the water drops or bits of ice get big, they fall to Earth as rain or snow.

rain falling

 What are clouds made of?

Think, Talk, and Write

1. **Make Predictions.** Would the ground feel hotter on a sunny day or a cloudy day?

2. Write about what the Sun does for us.

Health Link

Stand up and act out how water goes from the land up into the air. Reach up to the sky.

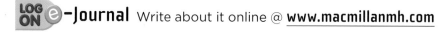

Weather Story

Look at this picture.
What do you think happened?
What do you think the boy is feeling?
What do you think he wanted to do?

 Write a Story
Write a story about this boy.
Make sure to write about the
weather in your story.

Remember
A story has a
clear beginning,
middle, and end.

 e-Journal Write about it online @ **www.macmillanmh.com**

 ELA W 1.2.1. Write brief narratives (e.g., fictional, autobiographical)
describing an experience.

Weather Graph

Anna asks her friends which activity they like best on warm, sunny days. She makes a bar graph to show what she finds out.

Sunny Day Activities

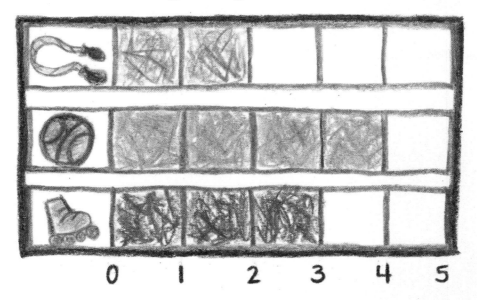

0   1   2   3   4   5

Make a Graph

Ask your friends which rainy day activity they like best. Make a bar graph to show what you find out.

Remember

A bar graph shows a picture of your information.

MA SDAP I.I.2. Represent and compare data (e.g., largest, smallest, most often, least often) by using pictures, bar graphs, tally charts, and picture graphs.

169
EXTEND

Measure Weather

Death Valley National Park, California

Look and Wonder

The Sun heats air, land, and water. Air can be very hot in the desert. What is the temperature here?

 I ES 3.a. Students know how to use simple tools (e.g., thermometer, wind vane) to measure weather conditions and record changes from day to day and across the seasons.

Explore

Inquiry Activity

What is the temperature outside today?

What to Do

① **Observe.** Look at a thermometer.

② **Record Data.** What is the temperature outside?

Explore More

③ **Predict.** Do you think the temperature outside is higher or lower than the temperature inside? How could you find out?

 I IE 4.b. Record observations and data with pictures, numbers, or written statements.

You need

thermometer

Step ②

Vocabulary

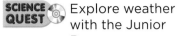

thermometer
rain gauge
wind vane

SCIENCE QUEST Explore weather with the Junior Rangers.

How can you measure weather?

You can use tools to measure weather. There are many kinds of tools for weather. Some tools measure temperature. Other tools measure wind and rain.

▼ **These children are measuring rainfall with a rain gauge.**

A **thermometer** measures the temperature of air and water.

A **rain gauge** measures how much rain falls.

A **wind vane** shows the direction of the wind.

 How do weather tools help us?

How can you learn more about the weather?

Scientists use tools to measure weather just like you. They use the information they collect to make weather reports.

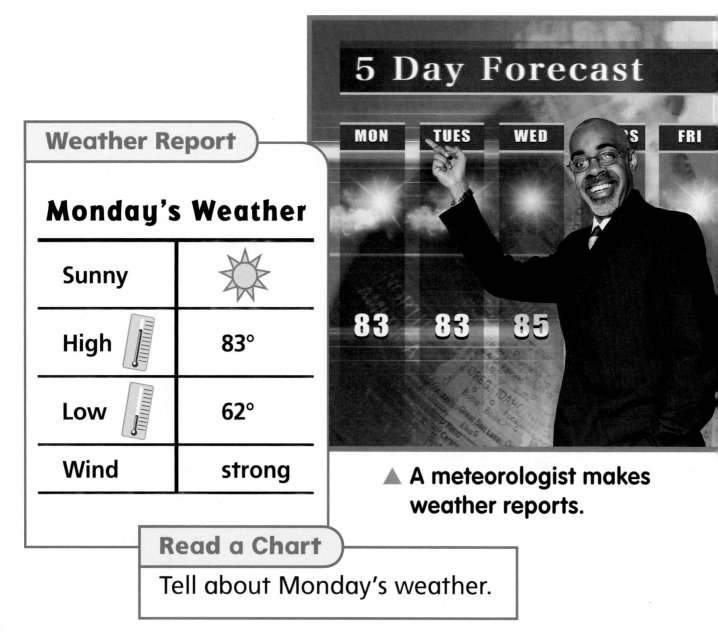

Weather Report

Monday's Weather

Sunny	☀
High	83°
Low	62°
Wind	strong

5 Day Forecast

| MON | TUES | WED | | FRI |

83 83 85

▲ A meteorologist makes weather reports.

Read a Chart

Tell about Monday's weather.

You can read weather reports in the newspaper. You can watch weather reports on television. You can even find weather reports on the computer.

✓ **Why do you think people care about the weather?**

Think, Talk, and Write

1. **Make Predictions.** What do you think the temperature is outside?

2. Write a weather report about today's weather.

Social Studies Link

How does weather affect your community?

Be a Scientist

You need

craft stick

streamer

tape

jar

thermometer

ruler

What is the weather like this week?

Find out if the weather changes from day to day.

What to Do

1. Make a wind vane and a rain gauge.

2. **Measure.** Take your wind vane, rain gauge, and a thermometer outside. Record what you find.

wind vane

rain gauge

Step 2

1 IE 4.b. Record observations and data with pictures, numbers, or written statements.

3 **Communicate.** Make a weather calendar. Observe and record the weather every day for one week. Use your weather tools.

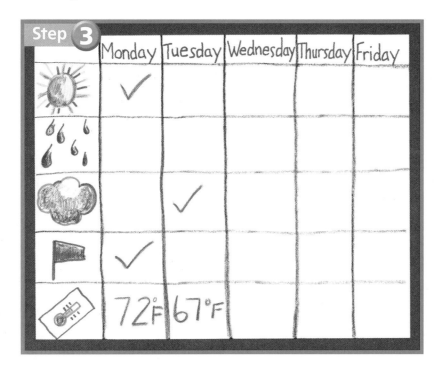

4 **Predict.** What will the weather be like next week?

Investigate More

Compare. Record the weather for another week. Does the weather change from day to day?

Weather Tool

A satellite is a tool that looks down on Earth from space.

It takes pictures of the planet. The pictures show where it is cloudy and where it is clear. Meteorologists are scientists who study the weather. Satellite pictures help them predict the weather.

The satellite pictures on the next page show one day of weather in California.

▶ **a satellite in space**

ELA R I.2.0. Students read and understand grade-level-appropriate material.

8:00 A.M.

▶ In the morning, a storm is moving over the ocean.

2:00 P.M.

▶ By afternoon, the storm has moved over the coast.

Talk About It

Make Predictions. Look at the clouds in the pictures. Where do you think the storm will go next?

LOG ON **e-Journal** Write about it online @ www.macmillanmh.com

AMERICAN
MUSEUM OF
NATURAL
HISTORY

My Weather Book

Drip! Drop!

Rain is falling.

Will it go away?

Splish! Splash!

The ground is wet.

Will it rain all day?

Look at this!

Here comes the Sun.

Let's go out and play.

The Sun is out.

The rain has stopped.

It is a sunny day.

What is this?

The ground is dry.

Where did the water go?

It went up into the sky.

It may come back as snow!

Vocabulary

weather, page 156

temperature, page 158

wind, page 159

thermometer, page 173

Fill in the blanks with one of the words.

1. Sunny, rainy, cloudy, and cold are words that describe _____. I ES 3

2. When you describe how hot or cold the air is, you are talking about _____. I ES 3.b

3. These trees show _____. I ES 3

4. This is a _____. I ES 3.a

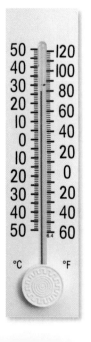

5. Does the Sun warm the land and air? How do you know? I ES 3.c

6. Predict. What do you think will happen to the puddle in this picture? I ES 3.c

7. Make Predictions. What do you think the weather will be like tomorrow? Why? I ES 3.b

 What do you know about weather? I ES 3

CHAPTER 4

Use a Thermometer

People use special tools to measure the weather.

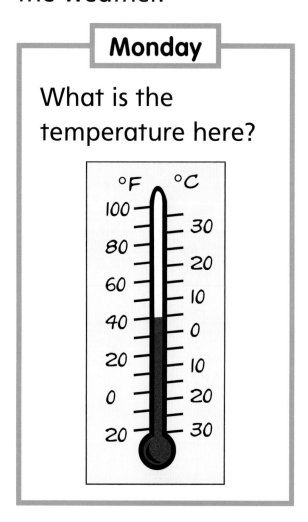

Monday

What is the temperature here?

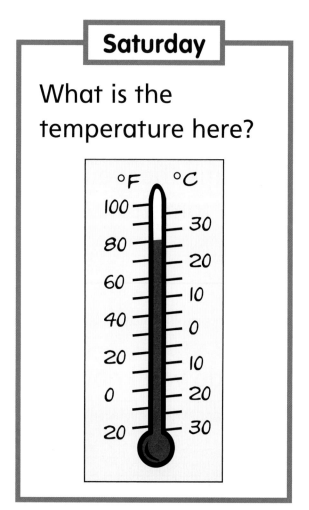

Saturday

What is the temperature here?

▶ Compare the temperatures. Which is hotter?

▶ What would you wear on Monday? What would you wear on Saturday?

 I ES 3.a. Students know how to use simple tools (e.g., thermometer, wind vane) to measure weather conditions and record changes from day to day and across the seasons.

1 You can measure changes in temperature with a _____. I ES 3.a

  A book

  B ruler

  C thermometer

  D hand lens

2 Use the diagram to answer the question.

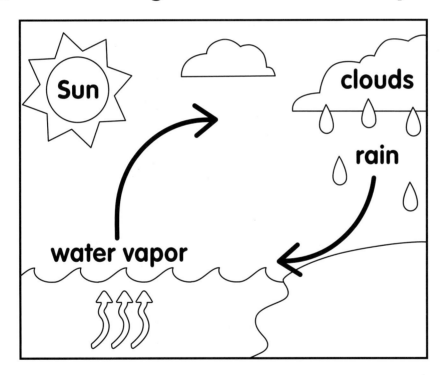

What warms the land and water? I ES 3.c

  A clouds

  B water

  C Sun

  D rain

Seasons

⭐ **What can you predict about the seasons?**

 I ES 3. Weather can be observed, measured, and described.

Literature
Poem

ELA R I.2.0. Students read and understand grade-level-appropriate material.

Sunflakes

by Frank Asch

If sunlight fell like snowflakes,
gleaming yellow and so bright,
we could build a sunman,
we could have a sunball fight,
we could watch the sunflakes
drifting in the sky.

We could go sleighing
in the middle of July
through sundrifts and sunbanks,
we could ride a sunmobile,
and we could touch sunflakes—
I wonder how they'd feel.

Talk About It

What would sunflakes
look like to you?

193

Winter

Look and Wonder

Does it snow everywhere in winter? Why or why not?

 1 ES 3.b. Students know that the weather changes from day to day but that trends in temperature or rain (or snow) tend to be predictable during a season.

What is winter weather like in different places?

What to Do

1. **Observe.** Look at the pictures showing winter in two California places, Lake Tahoe and San Diego.

2. **Compare.** How is winter weather different in different places?

3. **Record Data.** Write your ideas in a Venn diagram.

Explore More

4. **Communicate.** Tell what winter is like where you live.

Lake Tahoe

San Diego

 I IE 4.b. Record observations and data with pictures, numbers, or written statements.

Vocabulary

winter

season

How do you know when it is winter?

The air feels cold. It is winter. **Winter** is the coldest season. A **season** is a time of year. Winter, spring, summer, and fall are the four seasons of the year.

▲ In winter, it can be so cold that you might see your breath.

In winter, there are fewer hours of sunlight. The Sun has less time to warm the air, ground, and water. Less sunlight means plants have less energy to make food. Some plants die or lose their leaves.

Sunlight in Winter			
Date	**Sunrise**	**Sunset**	**Hours of Sunlight**
December 21	6:54 A.M.	4:47 P.M.	9 hours, 53 minutes

 What do you do in winter?

Read a Chart

Is it light outside if you wake up at 6:00 A.M.?

Carmel, California

◀ **In winter, it gets dark earlier.**

What is winter weather like?

Some places are colder than others. When winter is cold, there is not a lot of food for animals to eat. Some animals eat food they find. Others store food before winter begins so that they have food to eat.

squirrel

deer

In some places, it snows in winter. People wear coats to keep warm. In most places in California, it does not get cold enough to snow. It might rain a lot instead.

 What is winter weather like where you live?

Think, Talk, and Write

1. **Summarize.** What changes in winter?

2. Write about what you can see and do in winter where you live.

Health Link*

Draw or write about ways to stay safe in cold weather.

Record Data

When you **record data**, you write down information. You can keep track of the information you have found.

Learn It

The children in Miss Hayes' class made a tally chart to record data about their winter clothes.

I IE 4.b. Record observations and data with pictures, numbers, or written statements.

Try It

Look at the tally chart.

1. How many children in Miss Hayes' class are wearing coats?

2. How many children are wearing hats?

3. Make a tally chart about what your classmates wear to keep warm in winter.

Spring

Look and Wonder

In spring we see flowers. What helps them grow?

I ES 3.b. Students know that the weather changes from day to day but that trends in temperature or rain (or snow) tend to be predictable during a season.

What do seeds need to sprout?

What to Do

1. Put seeds on a dry and wet paper towel. Put each paper towel in a bag.

2. **Record Data.** Look at your seeds. Draw and write about what happens to the seeds.

Explore More

3. **Predict.** What would happen if you put the seeds in a freezer? Try it!

 I IE 4.b. Record observations and data with pictures, numbers, or written statements.

You need

seeds

paper towels

water

plastic zipper bags

Step **2**

Vocabulary

spring

How do you know when it is spring?

Look up into the sky! You might see butterflies. In spring you can see many animals. **Spring** is the season after winter.

▲ You can play outside after school because the sunlight lasts longer.

In spring, there are more hours of sunlight than in winter. The extra sunlight helps to warm the land, air, and water. People go outside more than they do in winter.

Date	Sunrise	Sunset	Hours of Sunlight
March 21	5:55 A.M.	6:04 P.M.	12 hours, 9 minutes

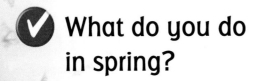 What do you do in spring?

Read a Chart

If you played outside until dark, what time would you have to come inside?

What happens in spring?

It takes longer for spring to come to places where the winters are very cold. When spring comes, the weather gets warmer. It might rain a lot. Rain and warmth from the Sun help plants grow.

▶ In spring, plants begin to sprout.

Growing plants are food for animals. Many animals are born in the spring. Some birds build nests for their young.

✓ What is spring like where you live?

birds' nest

Think, Talk, and Write

1. **Summarize.** What changes in spring?

2. Write about spring where you live.

Art Link

Draw a picture to show how living things change in spring.

Museum Mail Call

What is spring like in other places? Scientists at the American Museum of Natural History collect stories to learn about people around the world.

Dear Museum,

Be Méeybaan, how are you?

I live in Pakistan. My people, the Hunza, live in the mountains. It is April. Spring is here. We plant seeds and celebrate a spring festival. It does not rain much here.

The large, icy glaciers melt above our village as the weather gets warm each spring. We dig ditches so the water from the melted glaciers flows on our land. This helps our seeds grow.

From,

Nazir

  ELA R I.2.0. Students read and understand grade-level-appropriate material.

▼ The Hunza live high in the mountains.

Talk About It

Summarize. What happens in spring that helps the Hunza farmers' seeds grow?

LOG ON e-Journal Write about it online @ www.macmillanmh.com

California

Pakistan

Summer

Look and Wonder

The Sun is high in the sky in summer. Do you think some things get hotter than others in sunlight?

I ES 3.b. Students know that the weather changes from day to day but that trends in temperature or rain (or snow) tend to be predictable during a season.

Which does the Sun warm more?

What to Do

1. Place a cup of water and a cup of sand each in a sunny place.

2. **Compare.** Did the sand or water get hotter in the Sun?

3. **Record Data.** Write about your results.

Explore More

4. **Measure.** Repeat the activity using a thermometer. Were your results the same?

 I IE 4.b. Record observations and data with pictures, numbers, or written statements.

You need

cup of water

cup of sand

thermometer

Step 2

Vocabulary

summer

How do you know when it is summer?

You step outside and feel the hot Sun on your face. It is summer. **Summer** is the season after spring. People might spend more time outside in summer.

There are more hours of sunlight in summer than in any other season. Some animals have adapted to the hot Sun. Other animals look for shade to stay cool.

 What do you like to do in summer?

Summer Sunlight			
Date	**Sunrise**	**Sunset**	**Hours of Sunlight**
June 21	5:41 A.M.	8:07 P.M.	14 hours, 26 minutes

Read a Chart

If you woke up at 7 A.M. would it be light outside?

What is summer weather like?

In most places in California, it is hot and dry in the summer. Deserts have very hot summers.

California

Shasta Lake

Death Valley

▼ **Death Valley is the hottest and driest place in California.**

Summers might be cooler near the water or in the forest.

California

Shasta Lake

Death Valley

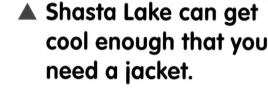

▲ Shasta Lake can get cool enough that you need a jacket.

 What is summer like where you live?

Think, Talk, and Write

1. **Summarize.** What changes in summer?

2. Write about summer in the desert and the forest.

Health Link

Why do you need to wear sunblock when you are outside?

Seasons Change

Look closely at the pictures. What is the same in each picture? What is different? What season does each picture show?

✏ Write About It

Write about one of the pictures. Describe the weather and what you think it would feel like if you were there.

Remember

Descriptive writing tells what something looks, feels, or sounds like.

LOG ON ℮-Journal Write about it online @ **www.macmillanmh.com**

 ELA W 1.1.2. Use descriptive words when writing.

Rain Table

Ethan lives in California. He recorded data about rainy days where he lives.

Month	Rainy Days
January	10
February	9
March	8
April	5
May	3
June	1
July	0
August	0
September	1
October	3
November	7
December	9

Read the Table

How many rainy days were there in June, July, and August? Add them up. What season do you think it is?

Remember
A table shows data in an organized way.

MA NS I.2.7. Find the sum of three one-digit numbers.

217
EXTEND

Fall

Look and Wonder

Some trees lose their leaves in the fall. How have the leaves in the picture changed?

I ES 3.b. Students know that the weather changes from day to day but that trends in temperature or rain (or snow) tend to be predictable during a season.

How do leaves change in the seasons?

What to Do

① **Observe.** Look at the pictures of leaves in different seasons.

② **Compare.** How are the leaves alike? How are they different?

③ **Record Data.** Draw and color the leaves. Write the season when you might see each leaf.

Explore More

④ **Communicate.** What happens to leaves in different seasons where you live?

 I IE 4.b. Record observations and data with pictures, numbers, or written statements.

Vocabulary

fall

How do you know when it is fall?

Sometimes the air feels cooler and the wind blows stronger. **Fall** is the season after summer. Some leaves change color in the fall.

aspens in summer

aspens in fall

In fall, there are fewer hours of sunlight than in summer. Less sunlight makes the temperature cooler. Some places in California stay warm all year. In these places the leaves do not change color.

Date	Sunrise	Sunset	Hours of Sunlight
September 22	6:40 A.M.	6:50 P.M.	12 hours, 10 minutes

 What is fall like in California?

palms in summer

palms in fall

What happens in fall?

In many places it rains more in fall than in summer. In fall, many animals begin storing food for winter. Some animals move to warmer places.

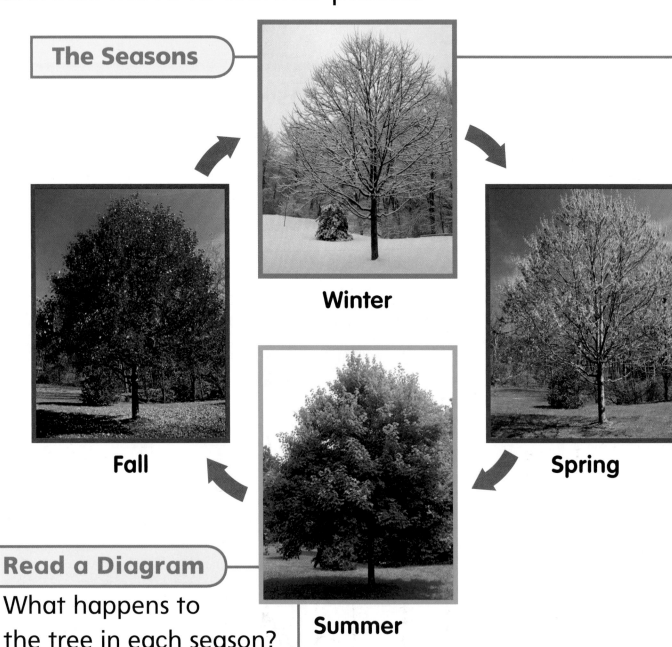

The Seasons

Winter

Spring

Fall

Summer

Read a Diagram

What happens to the tree in each season?

LOG ON *Science in Motion* Watch the four seasons @ **www.macmillanmh.com**

Some fruits get ripe in the fall. People can pick the fruits and eat them.

 What is fall like where you live?

Think, Talk, and Write

1. **Summarize.** What changes in fall?

2. Write how fall and spring are different where you live.

Social Studies Link*

Describe how each season affects what people do.

LOG ON e-**Review** Summaries and quizzes online @ **www.macmillanmh.com**

pumpkin patch

You need

newspapers

paper

pencil

How many hours of sunlight are there in a day?

Find out how the amount of sunlight changes over a week.

What to Do

1 Find the chart in a newspaper that tells the time of sunrise and sunset.

2 **Record Data.** Write the times of sunrise and sunset each day for a week on a chart.

Date	Sunrise	Sunset
Monday	7:00 A.M.	6:16 P.M.
Tuesday	7:00 A.M.	6:14 P.M.
Wednesday	7:01 A.M.	6:13 P.M.
Thursday	7:02 A.M.	6:12 P.M.
Friday	7:03 A.M.	6:11 P.M.

 1 IE 4.b. Record observations and data with pictures, numbers, or written statements.

3 **Draw Conclusions.** How did the amount of sunlight change in a week?

Step **3**

Day	Sunrise	Sunset
Monday		
Tuesday		
Wednesday		
Thursday		
Friday		

Investigate More
Predict. Will sunrise happen earlier or later next week?

My Seasons Book

Winter, spring, summer, fall,

One after the other,

I like them all!

Winter can be cold.

I need my mittens.

I like to play in the snow.

Spring can be wet.

I need my rain boots.

I like all of the flowers.

Summer can be sunny.

I need my hat.

I like to play in the sand.

Fall can be cool.

I need my jacket.

I like to play in the leaves.

Winter, spring, summer, fall,

One after the other,

I like them all!

Vocabulary

winter, page 196

spring, page 204

summer, page 212

fall, page 220

What does each picture show?

1

2

I ES 3.b

I ES 3.b

3

4

I ES 3.b

I ES 3.b

5. Write about the season in the picture below. I ES 3.b

6. Record Data. Write about how the seasons change where you live. I ES 3.b

7. Summarize. Use a summary chart to tell what you learned about winter. I ES 3.b

⭐ What can you predict about the seasons? I ES 3

CHAPTER 5

Draw the Seasons

▶ Fold a piece of paper in half and then in half again.

▶ Draw a picture to show what happens in each season.

▶ Write a sentence below each picture that describes the weather in that season.

I ES 3.b. Students know that the weather changes from day to day but that trends in temperature or rain (or snow) tend to be predictable during a season.

1 **This diagram shows the seasons.**

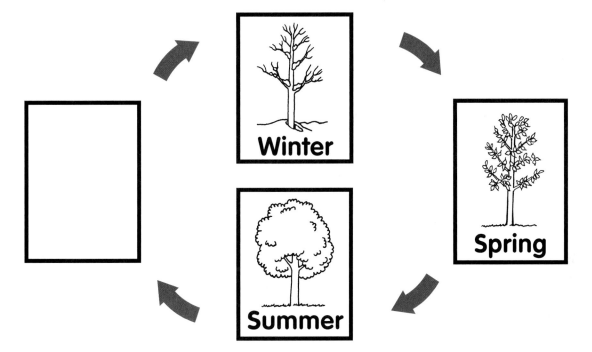

Which season is missing? I ES 3.b

A spring

B winter

C summer

D fall

2 **Which season has the most hours of sunlight?** I ES 3.b

A spring

B winter

C summer

D fall

Weather and WILD ANIMALS

What do animals do in different kinds of weather? Let's find out!

Hot

This elephant knows just the thing for a hot day—a cool bath!

▼ **elephant bathing**

Cold

It is a cold, snowy day.
This fox curls up.
It uses its bushy tail
as a blanket.

▲ **arctic fox curling up**

Rainy

Here comes the rain! The
butterfly hides under
a leaf. It hangs upside
down to stay dry.

▲ **butterfly hiding**

Sunny

This turtle lies in the
Sun to get warm.

▲ **turtle lying in the Sun**

 ELA R I.2.0. Students read and understand grade-level-appropriate material.

Storm Chaser

Do you like watching it rain? You could become a storm chaser. They try to get close to storms in order to learn how they work.

Storm chasers study the weather. They use weather tools when studying a storm.

It is very important for storm chasers to know how to stay safe in a storm.

storm chaser

More careers for people who like weather.

weather reporter

relief worker

Physical Science

Heating the air makes the balloons rise.

Solids, Liquids, and Gases

★ What is the world made of?

 I PS I. Materials come in different forms (states), including solids, liquids, and gases.

Literature
Poem

ELA R I.2.0. Students read and understand grade-level-appropriate material.

Our World

by Meish Goldish

The grass is green,
The sky is blue,
The moon is white,
The clouds are, too.

The sun is yellow,
The trees are brown,
The leaves are red
When falling down.
The sunset's orange,
The air is clear,
What a colorful world
We have right here!

Talk About It

What words are used to
describe our world? How
would you describe our world?

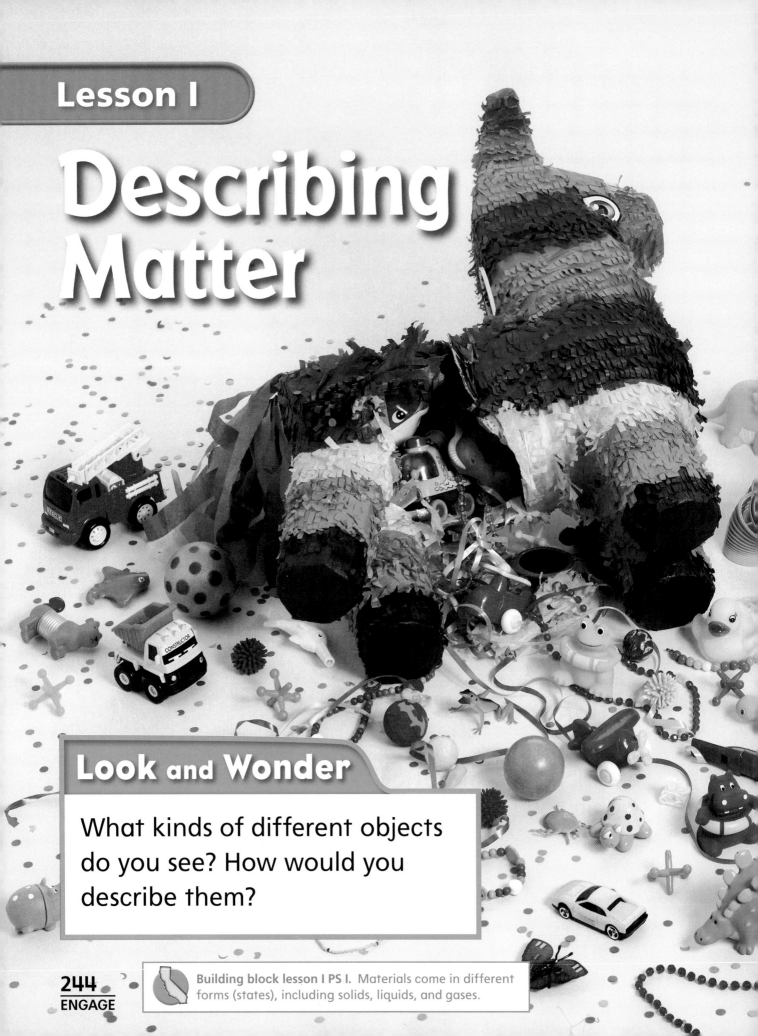

Describing Matter

Look and Wonder

What kinds of different objects do you see? How would you describe them?

Building block lesson 1 PS 1. Materials come in different forms (states), including solids, liquids, and gases.

How can you describe an object?

What to Do

1 **Observe.** Look at a cracker. Now use a hand lens. What more do you see?

crackers

hand lens

2 **Communicate.** Draw a picture of what you observed. Share your picture with a partner.

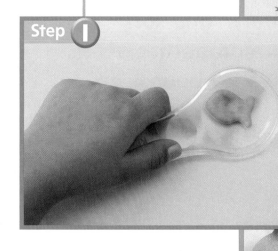

Step **1**

3 **Measure.** Look at other crackers. Are they all the same size? How do you know?

Explore More

4 **Infer.** How can you change the cracker?

 I IE 4.a. Draw pictures that portray some features of the thing being described.

Vocabulary

properties
matter
states of matter
mass
balance

What are the properties of matter?

When you describe something, you talk about its properties. **Properties** are how something looks, feels, smells, or tastes. Color, size, and shape are also properties.

▼ Brown and soft are properties of this toy bear.

Every kind of matter has its own properties. **Matter** is what all things are made up of. Matter comes in three forms. They are solid, liquid, and gas. These forms are called **states of matter**.

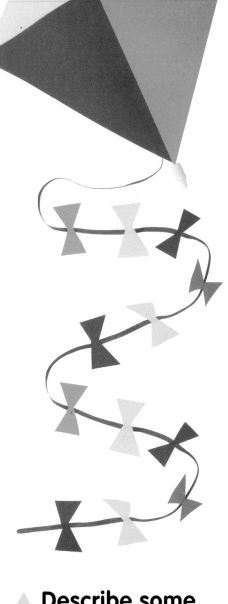

✓ What is matter?

▼ **The water, the raft, and the people are all matter.**

▲ **Describe some properties of the kite.**

What is mass?

All matter takes up space. The metal bear takes up less space than the sponge bear. **Mass** is how much matter is in an object. Heavier things have more mass than lighter things.

Big Bear, Little Bear

Read a Photo

Which object has more mass? How do you know?

A **balance** can be used to measure mass.

balance

✓ Which car do you think has more mass? Why?

Think, Talk, and Write

1. **Cause and Effect.** If you put books in a backpack, would the properties of the backpack change?

2. Write about and draw a picture of your shirt. Describe its properties.

Math Link

What has more mass than an apple? Use a balance to find out.

Measure

You **measure** to find out the size or amount of something. You can use string or cubes to measure how long or wide something is.

Learn It

Whitney used cubes to compare the length of three books. She made a chart to show what she found out.

How Long Is a Book?

I Spy	13 cubes
The Biggest Tree	8 cubes
Watch It Grow	8 cubes

 MA MG I.I.I. Compare the length, weight, and volume of two or more objects by using direct comparison or a nonstandard unit.

Try It

Look at the pictures below.

 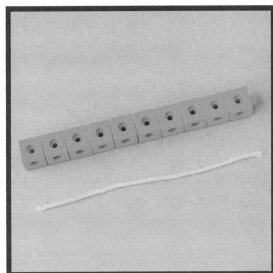

1. How many cubes wide is the can in the picture?

2. Use string to measure the width of two classroom objects. How many cubes wide is each object?

3. Make a chart to show what you find out.

Solids

Sierra Nevada, California

Look and Wonder

There are many different kinds of matter on Earth. How would you describe the properties of these rocks?

I PS I.a. Students know solids, liquids, and gases have different properties.

What are some properties of solids?

1. Collect different rocks.

2. **Classify.** Sort them by their properties.

3. **Measure.** Use a balance to find out which rocks have more mass.

Explore More

4. **Infer.** Can you do anything to change the shape of the rocks? Why or why not?

 I IE 4.e. Make new observations when discrepancies exist between two descriptions of the same object or phenomenon.

You need

rocks

hand lens

balance

Step 1

Vocabulary

solid

texture

 SCIENCE QUEST Explore properties of solids with the Junior Rangers.

What is a solid?

A **solid** is a state of matter that has a shape of its own. This boy is building with solid, wooden blocks.

Center Time

Read a Photo

Describe the solids in this picture.

The amount of matter in a solid always stays the same. If you take apart a puzzle, the amount of matter in the puzzle does not change.

 What are some solids? What are their properties?

What are the properties of solids?

Solids have many different properties. They can be large or small. They come in many different shapes and colors. You can fold and bend some solids.

How an object feels is its **texture**. Solids might feel smooth or rough.

 How would you describe some of these solids?

Think, Talk, and Write

1. **Cause and Effect.** If you cut a piece of paper, do you have the same amount of matter?

2. Write a list of solids that bend.

Art Link

Use solid materials with different textures to make a collage. What does it feel like?

A Shoe Story

Look at Manny's shoes. Where do you think they have been?

✏ Write About It

Write a story about Manny's shoes and where they have been. Describe the properties of the shoes.

Remember
A story has a clear beginning, middle, and end.

 **e-Journal** Write about it online @ **www.macmillanmh.com**

 ELA W 1.2.1. Write brief narratives (e.g., fictional, autobiographical) describing an experience.

Pieces of Matter

Eva wonders if she will have the same amount of matter if she cuts a 20 inch ribbon into three pieces. She measures the length of each piece.

2 inches

6 inches

12 inches

Eva writes a number sentence to show what she finds out.

$$2 + 6 + 12 = 20$$

Write a Number Sentence

Cut a 12 inch piece of string into three pieces. Write a number sentence to show that the amount of matter has not changed.

> **Remember**
> A number sentence helps you solve a problem.

MA AF I.I.I. Write and solve number sentences from problem situations that express relationships involving addition and subtraction.

Liquids

Look and Wonder

This boy is swimming in water. How would you describe the properties of water?

 I PS I.a. Students know solids, liquids, and gases have different properties.

What are the properties of a liquid?

You need

1. **Measure.** Fill a dropper with colored water. Place drops next to each other on wax paper.

colored water

2. **Observe.** Use a toothpick to change the position of the drops. What happens?

wax paper

Explore More

3. **Infer.** Do liquids have their own shape? How do you know?

dropper

toothpicks

 I IE 4.d. Describe the relative position of objects by using two references (e.g., above and next to, below and left of).

Step 1

Vocabulary
liquid

What is a liquid?

A **liquid** is a state of matter. Liquids have mass and take up space like solids. They do not have a shape of their own. Liquids flow and take the shape of whatever they are in.

▼ Liquids flow. This water is flowing into a lake.

Middle Falls, McCloud River, California

A liquid's shape might look different in different containers, but the amount of liquid stays the same.

✔ What are the properties of some liquids?

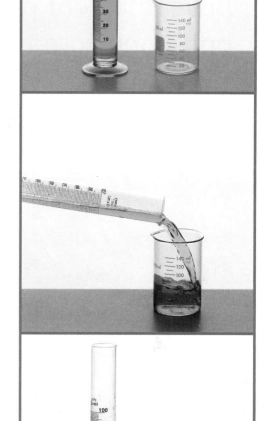

Read a Photo

Is the amount of liquid the same in each picture?

What are the properties of different liquids?

There are some properties that all liquids have. Different liquids can have different properties. Mustard and honey are thick liquids. They flow slowly.

mustard

honey

milk

shampoo

oil

dish soap

Milk and water are thin liquids.
They flow fast.

 What are some properties of milk
and water?

water

Think, Talk, and Write

1. **Cause and Effect.** What happens to
   the shape of a liquid if you spill it?

2. Write a list of thick liquids.

Math Link

Put molasses and water each in a bag.
Compare how each liquid moves. Which
has more mass?

Be a Scientist

You need

dish soap

honey

ketchup

mustard

teaspoon

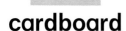

cardboard

Which liquid flows the fastest?

Find out the properties of different liquids.

What to Do

1 **Predict.** Which liquid will flow the fastest? Which will flow the slowest?

2 **Measure.** Place a teaspoon of each liquid on one end of a piece of cardboard.

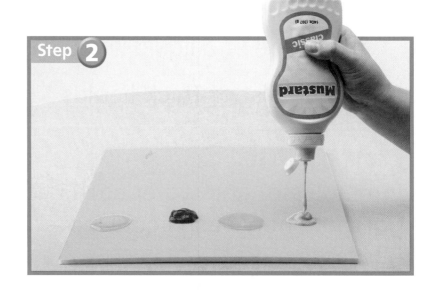

Step 2

I IE 4.d. Describe the relative position of objects by using two references (e.g., above and next to, below and left of).

3 **Compare.** Slowly lift the edge of the cardboard. Compare the positions of the liquids as they move.

Step **3**

4 **Record Data.** Use the chart below to record the speed of each liquid.

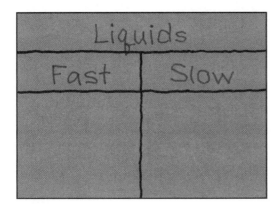

Liquids

Fast	Slow

Investigate More

Classify. Repeat the experiment with different liquids.

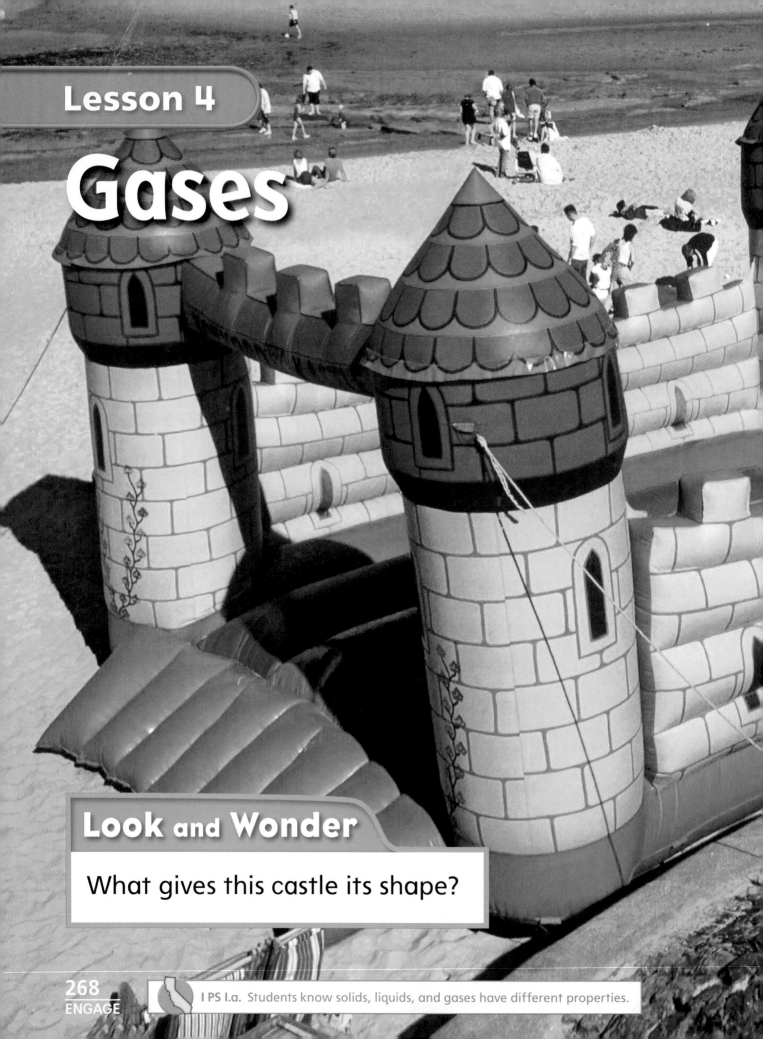

Gases

Look and Wonder

What gives this castle its shape?

I PS I.a. Students know solids, liquids, and gases have different properties.

What is in the cup?

1. Push an empty cup to the bottom of a pan of colored water.

2. **Communicate.** What happens?

3. **Infer.** Why do you think the water does not fill the cup?

Explore More

4. **Measure.** Add one cup of water to the pan. Did adding water change your results?

 I IE 4.e. Make new observations when discrepancies exist between two descriptions of the same object or phenomenon.

You need

plastic cup

food coloring

plastic bin

Step 1

Vocabulary

gas

What is a gas?

Gas is a state of matter. Just like liquids, gas does not have its own shape. Unlike liquids, gas spreads out to fill the space of whatever it is in.

◀ **These balloons are filled with gas that gives them their shape.**

The air we breathe is made up of different gases. You can not see the gases, but you can feel them.

✓ What are the properties of gases?

▶ These wind socks are filled with air.

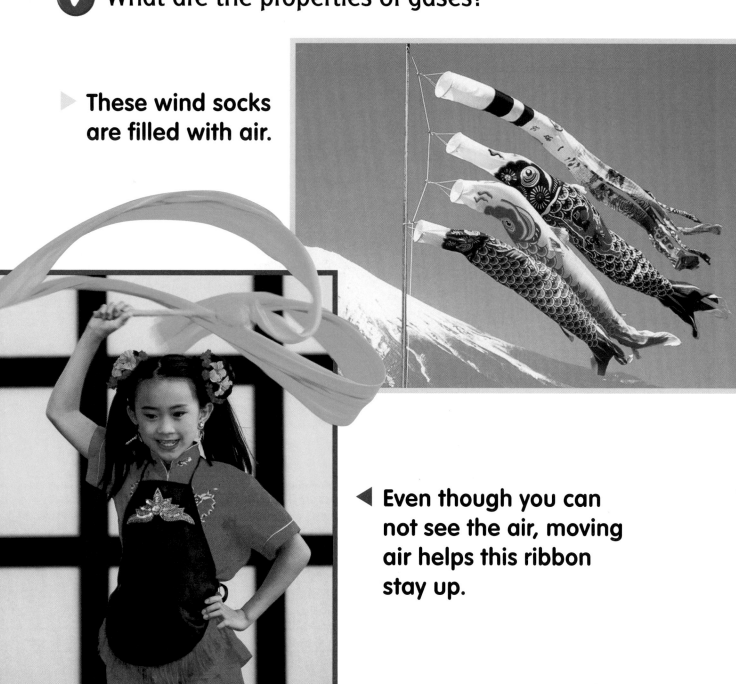

◀ Even though you can not see the air, moving air helps this ribbon stay up.

What are some properties of gases?

Gas spreads out evenly until it can not spread any more. Gas can flow up, down, and all around.

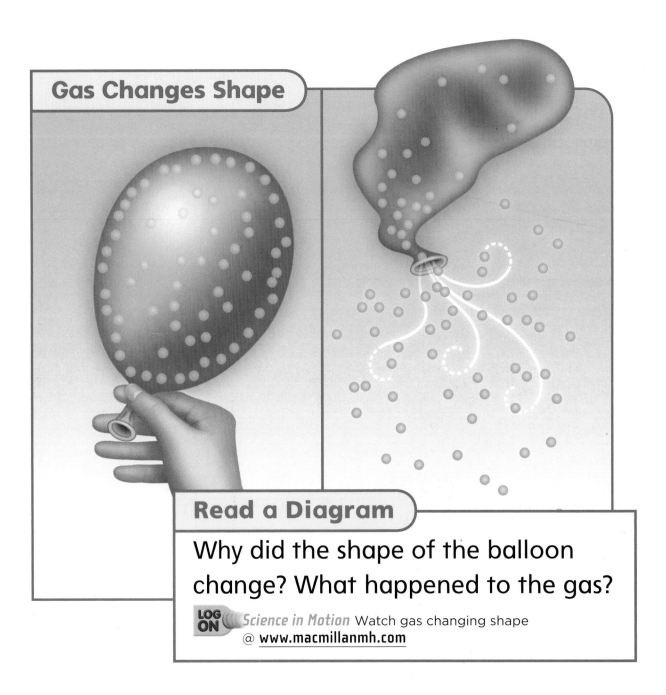

Gas Changes Shape

Read a Diagram

Why did the shape of the balloon change? What happened to the gas?

LOG ON *Science in Motion* Watch gas changing shape @ **www.macmillanmh.com**

When you blow into a ball, gas fills the inside. As gas fills up the space inside the ball, it gives the ball its shape.

✓ What would happen to the gas in a balloon if it had a hole?

Think, Talk, and Write

1. **Cause and Effect.** What happens if you push a balloon into a pan of water?

2. Write what happens when you blow air into a balloon.

Art Link

Draw a picture that includes solids, liquids, and gases.

Blimps

How do blimps float in the sky? Blimps are filled with helium just like some balloons. Helium is a gas that is lighter than air. The helium makes the blimp float.

▲ Long ago, blimps had dining rooms for 100 passengers.

100 Years Ago

Some people used blimps to travel from place to place, even across the Atlantic Ocean.

 ELA R I.2.0. Students read and understand grade-level-appropriate material.

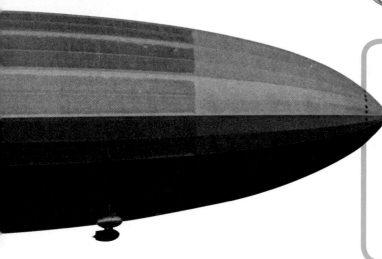

Talk About It

Cause and Effect. How does the helium help a blimp stay in the air?

LOG ON e-**Journal** Write about it online @ **www.macmillanmh.com**

Today

Blimps fly over sports' stadiums. They take pictures of games.

Would you like to fly in a blimp? Where would you go?

▲ **Today, blimps can only carry seven or eight passengers.**

My Matter Book

What is matter?

There are three states it could be.

Solid, liquid, or gas,

what kinds of matter do you see?

A rock is a solid.

It can be rough or smooth.

It keeps its shape,
even if moved.

Water is a liquid.

It moves fast or slow.

It changes its shape
wherever it goes.

Air is a gas.

It is hard to see.

When let out,
it spreads evenly.

The earth is matter.

So is the sea.

The air is matter,

like you and me.

Vocabulary

matter, page 247

mass, page 248

solid, page 254

liquid, page 262

What kind of matter does each picture show?

I PS I.a

I PS I.a

Use these pictures to complete the sentences.

3. The bears are made of _____. I PS I.a

4. The sponge bear has less _____ than the metal bear. I PS I.a

5. What does the picture below show about the properties of gases? I PS I.a

6. Measure. What are ways to measure a solid? I PS I.a

7. Cause and Effect. How could you change the shape of a liquid? I PS I.a

⭐ What is the world made up of? I PS I

CHAPTER 6

All Kinds of Matter

Everything around you is matter.

▶ Make a chart like the one below.

▶ Find pictures of solids, liquids, and gases to put on the chart.

▶ Label the pictures.

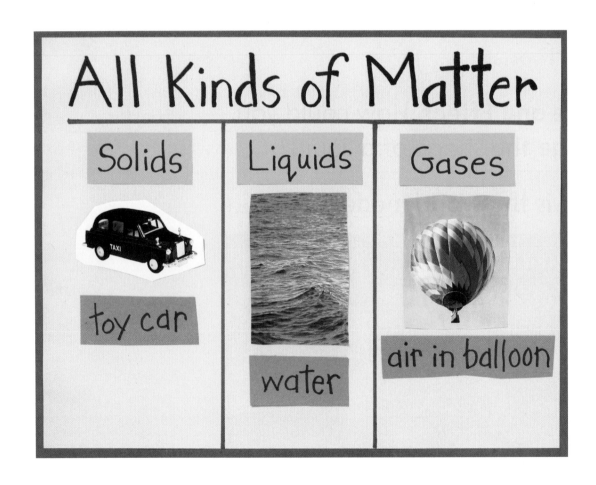

I PS I. Materials come in different forms (states), including solids, liquids, and gases.

1 Which kind of matter has a shape of its own? I PS I.a

   A gas

   B water

   C liquid

   D solid

2 This picture shows a balloon.

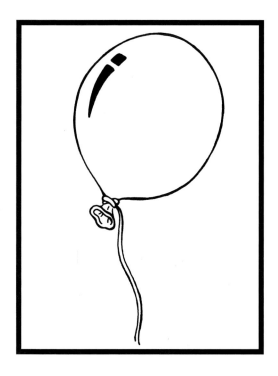

What fills this balloon? I PS I.a

   A solid

   B nothing

   C gas

   D liquid

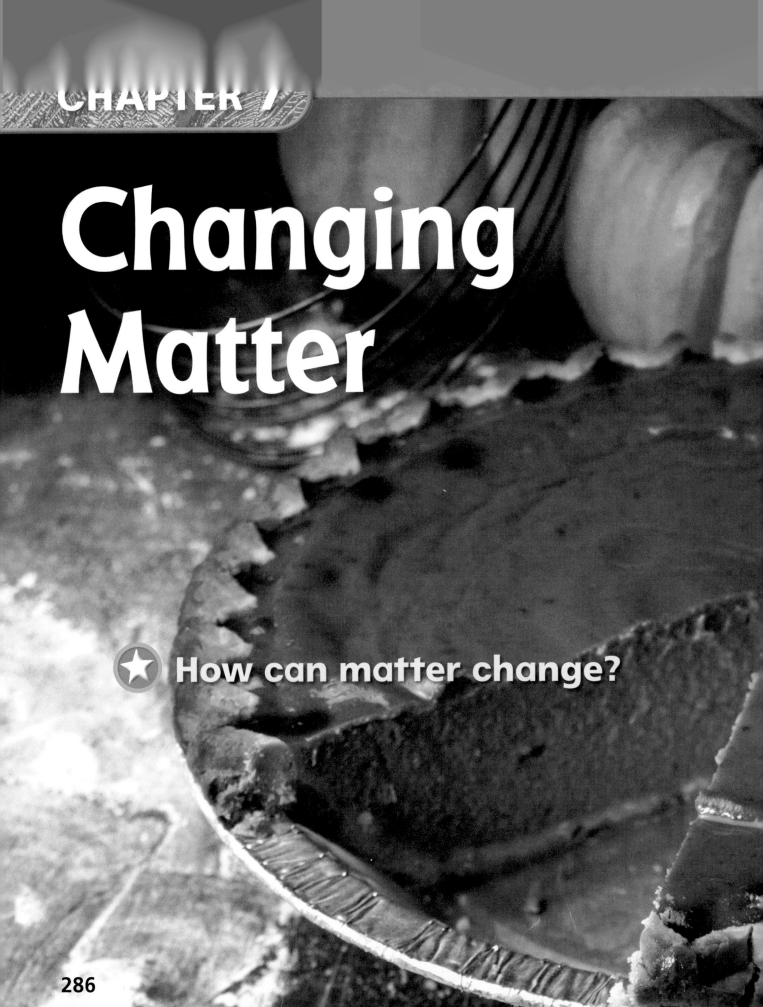

Changing Matter

★ How can matter change?

I PS I. Materials come in different forms (states), including solids, liquids, and gases.

287

Popcorn Hop

by Stephanie Calmenson

Everybody do
the popcorn dance!

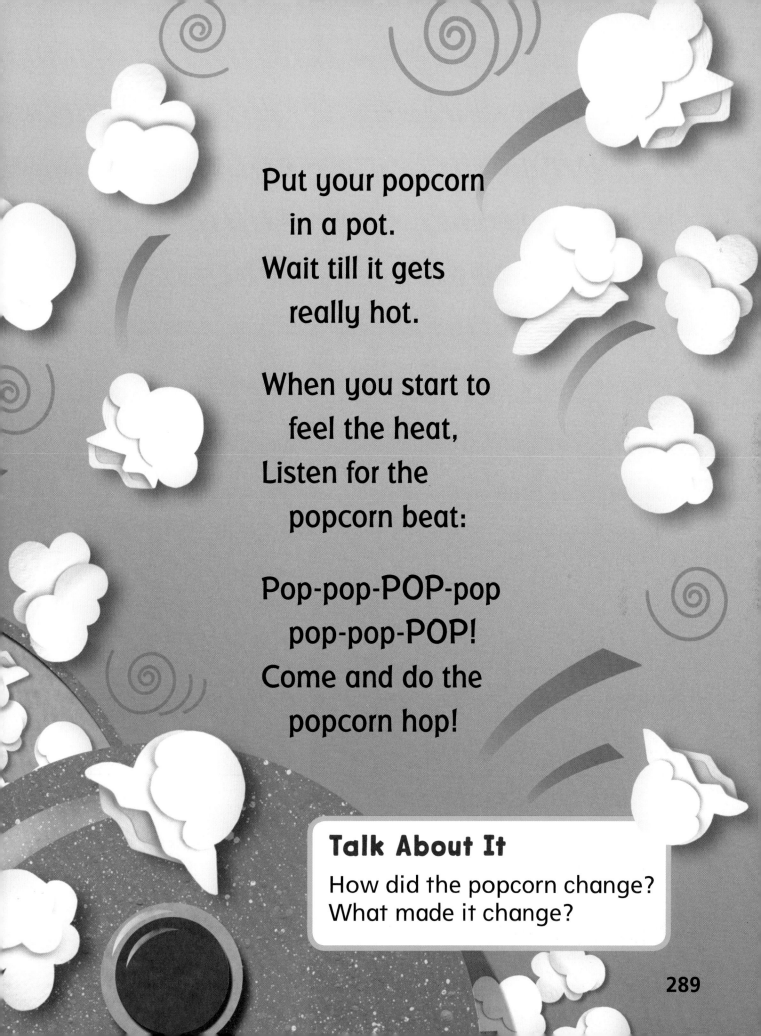

Put your popcorn
in a pot.
Wait till it gets
really hot.

When you start to
feel the heat,
Listen for the
popcorn beat:

Pop-pop-POP-pop
pop-pop-POP!
Come and do the
popcorn hop!

Talk About It

How did the popcorn change?
What made it change?

289

Heating Matter

Look and Wonder

The lava that flows from a volcano is melted rock. How do you think rocks melt?

 1 PS 1.b. Students know the properties of substances can change when the substances are mixed, cooled, or heated.

How can heat change water?

What to Do

① **Measure.** Take the temperature inside a cup with ice cubes. Then place the cup in a sunny place.

② **Observe.** Wait 10 minutes. How did the ice cubes change?

③ **Measure.** Take the temperature inside the cup again. How has the temperature changed?

Explore More

④ **Put Things in Order.** Write what happened to the ice cubes.

You need

cup with ice cubes

thermometer

Step ①

Vocabulary

melting

evaporates

boiling

SCIENCE QUEST Explore how heat can change matter with the Junior Rangers.

How does heat change a solid?

When solids get enough heat, they melt. **Melting** means to change from a solid to a liquid.

◄ When ice melts, it changes from a solid to a liquid.

▶ Cheese melts when it is heated.

Solids can melt with a
little or with a lot of heat.

✔ **What are other
solids that melt?**

▲ **Heat makes candle
wax melt.**

▼ **Glass blowers use a lot of
heat to change the shape
of glass.**

How can heat change a liquid?

When water is heated, some water **evaporates**, or goes into the air as gas.

▼ **What will happen to this cup of water in a week?**

Day 1

Day 2

Day 5

Heat from the Sun made the water in this soil evaporate.

When a liquid gets enough heat, it boils. **Boiling** can change a liquid to a gas.

Boiling Water

Read a Photo

How do you know this water is boiling?

✓ What happens when water evaporates?

Think, Talk, and Write

1. **Put Things in Order.** Describe how heat can change water.

2. Write about what happens to ice cream on a sunny day.

Social Studies Link

What would you need to do to sell juice pops on a hot summer day?

LOG ON e-Review Summaries and quizzes online @ www.macmillanmh.com

Put Things in Order

You **put things in order** when you tell what comes first, next, and last.

Peggy cooked spaghetti. She made a chart to show the steps.

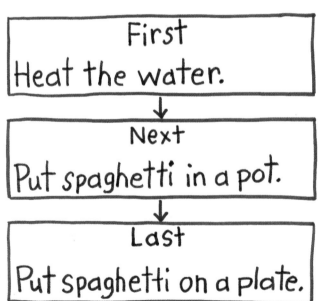

First
Heat the water.

↓

Next
Put spaghetti in a pot.

↓

Last
Put spaghetti on a plate.

 I IE 4.b. Record observations and data with pictures, numbers, or written statements.

Try It

Look at the picture below.

1. What is happening in this picture?

2. What do you think will happen next?

3. Use a chart like Peggy's to show what came first, next, and last.

First
↓
Next
↓
Last

Cooling Matter

Look and Wonder

Why do you think some of this water is frozen?

  I PS I.b. Students know the properties of substances can change when the substances are mixed, cooled, or heated.

How does cooling change a liquid?

What to Do

① Fill a cup with water.

② **Measure.** Take the temperature of the water. Then put ice cubes in the cup.

③ **Measure.** Take the temperature of the water with ice after 10 minutes and then again after 20 minutes.

Explore More

④ **Put Things in Order.** Tell how you changed the temperature of the water.

 I IE 4.e. Make new observations when discrepancies exist between two descriptions of the same object or phenomenon.

You need

cup of water

ice cubes

thermometer

Step ②

Vocabulary

freeze
cooling

How can liquids change?

What happens to water when you put it in the freezer? When you **freeze** a liquid, it turns into a solid.

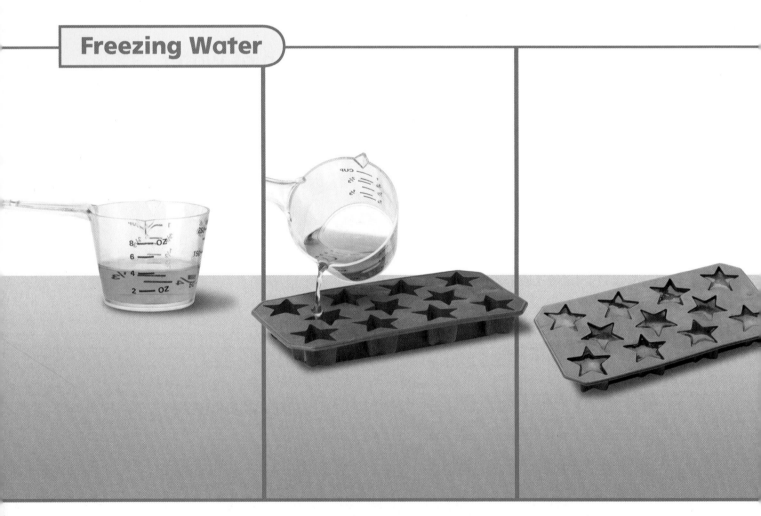

Freezing Water

▲ Liquid water takes the shape of its container. When you put water in a freezer, it becomes a solid.

You can change frozen water back
into a liquid. When you heat a
solid it melts.

▼ **When the ice melts, the water
in the cup is the water that you
started with before.**

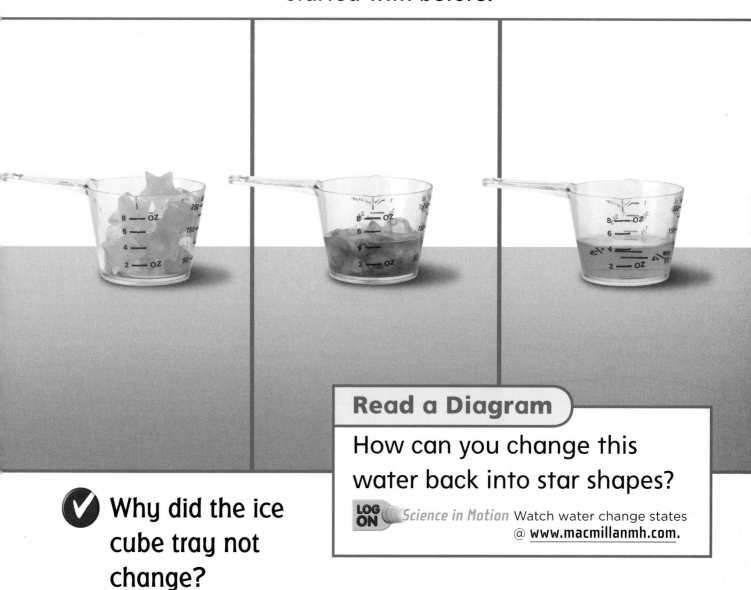

Read a Diagram

How can you change this
water back into star shapes?

LOG ON *Science in Motion* Watch water change states
@ **www.macmillanmh.com.**

✔ Why did the ice
cube tray not
change?

How can you cool matter?

Have you ever put a bottle of water
in the freezer? What happened?
When water is frozen it expands.
Frozen water takes up more space
than liquid water. When you freeze
a liquid, it turns into a solid.

▶ **As the water
freezes, it
expands.**

To make something freeze, you have to cool it. **Cooling** means to take heat away.

✓ What are other ways to cool soup?

▶ **This boy's breath is cooler than the hot soup.**

Think, Talk, and Write

1. **Put Things in Order.** Describe what happens to liquids when you cool them.

2. Write about what happens when you put a liquid in the freezer.

Math Link

Does a cup of water have the same mass as a cup of ice? Try it!

Meet Rondi Davies

Rondi Davies is a geologist at the American Museum of Natural History.

A geologist is a scientist who studies rocks. Rondi studies diamonds and how they were formed.

Diamonds are made of carbon. Heat and pressure deep inside Earth can change carbon into diamonds.

▲ **Rondi Davies**

uncut diamonds

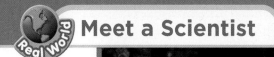
▶ **cut diamond**

If hot carbon cools very quickly, a diamond is formed.

If hot carbon cools slowly, graphite is formed. That's the gray tip of your pencil!

▲ **graphite**

Talk About It

Put Things in Order. How can carbon become a diamond?

 e-Journal Write about it online @ **www.macmillanmh.com**

 ELA R I.2.0. Students read and understand grade-level-appropriate material.

 AMERICAN MUSEUM OF NATURAL HISTORY

Lesson 3

Mixing Matter

Look and Wonder

When water evaporates from the ocean, what do you think happens to the salt in the water?

 I PS I.b. Students know the properties of substances can change when the substances are mixed, cooled, or heated.

What happens to salt in water?

What to Do

1 **Measure.** Mix four tablespoons of salt into one half cup of water.

2 Pour the mixture into a pan. Put the pan in a sunny place for a few days.

3 **Put Things in Order.** Write what happened first, next, and last.

Explore More

4 **Predict.** What would happen if you mix sugar instead of salt? Try it!

 I IE 4.b. Record observations and data with pictures, numbers, or written statements.

You need

pan

salt

water

Step **1**

Vocabulary

mixture
dissolve

What is a mixture?

A **mixture** is two or more different things put together. When you mix solids, you can see the different parts of the mixture. It is easy to pick them apart.

▲ You can easily separate the foods in this party mix.

▲ This fruit salad is a mixture, too. Can you separate its parts?

It is not as easy to separate solid and liquid mixtures. Some solids **dissolve**, or completely mix into a liquid.

✓ What other mixtures can be separated?

▶ This juice mix will dissolve in water.

What are other types of mixtures?

Sometimes when you mix things, it is not easy to get the objects back to what they originally were.

▼ **It is hard to take an egg out of milk once they have been mixed.**

When you cook, heat can change a mixture into something else.

Read a Photo

Can this breakfast be changed back to raw eggs and milk?

✓ What other mixtures can not easily be separated?

Think, Talk, and Write

1. **Put Things in Order.** Tell how you would cook a breakfast of scrambled eggs.

2. Write about a mixture. How was it made?

Health Link

Describe some foods that are mixtures.

Mix It Up!

Look at this picture.

What happened?

What are some things in this mixture?

✏️ **Write a Story**

Write a story about this mixture. Has this mixture made something new or can it be taken apart?

Remember

Use your sense of sight to tell how something looks.

 -Journal Write about it online @ **www.macmillanmh.com**

 I ELA W I.2.2. Write brief expository descriptions of a real object, person, place, or event using sensory details.

Trail Mix Recipe

Carrie made trail mix. She used this recipe and mixed everything together.

Carrie's Trail Mix
2 cups dried fruit
1 cup nuts
1 cup raisins

Write a Number Sentence

Make your own trail mix. Write a number sentence to show how many cups of different objects are in your mix.

Remember
A number sentence helps you solve a problem.

 MA AF 1.1.1. Write and solve number sentences from problem situations that express relationships involving addition and subtraction.

Be a Scientist

vinegar

baking soda

plastic bottle

funnel

balloon

What happens when you mix baking soda and vinegar?

Find out if they can be changed back.

What to Do

1 **Measure.** Put four teaspoons of vinegar into a plastic bottle.

△ **Be Careful.** Wear your safety goggles!

Step 1

2 **Measure.** Put one teaspoon of baking soda into a balloon.

Step 2

 I IE 4.b. Record observations and data with pictures, numbers, or written statements.

3 Stretch the balloon over the top of the bottle. Do not let the baking soda fall into the bottle.

4 **Observe.** Hold the balloon straight up so the baking soda falls into the bottle. What happens?

5 **Put Things in Order.** Write what happened first, next, and last.

Investigate More

Infer. Can you separate the baking soda from the vinegar? Why or why not?

Mix It Up

You can make many mixtures.

Some can be easily taken
apart. Others can not.

Fruit salad can be
easily taken apart.

Smoothies can not.

You can easily pick the
apple slices out of this pie.

But you can not easily take
the pumpkin out of this one!

Vocabulary

> **boiling**, page 295
>
> **melting**, page 292
>
> **mixture**, page 308
>
> **freeze**, page 300

Fill in the blanks.

1. The wax on the candle is _____. I PS I.b

2. This is a _____. I PS I.b

3. The water in the pot is _____. I PS I.b

4. When you turn water into a solid, you _____ it. I PS I.b

5. Tell how a juice pop can change from a solid to a liquid. I PS I.b

6. **Put Things in Order.** Tell how ice changes into a liquid and then changes back. I PS I.b

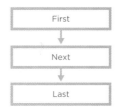

7. **Put Things in Order.** Tell how an egg can be changed into something different. I PS I.b

 How can matter change? I PS I

CHAPTER 7

Plan an Experiment

You can plan an experiment to answer a question.

▶ If a drink mix has been dissolved in water, can it become a powder again?

▶ Write down the steps of your experiment.

▶ Try it!

  I PS I.b. Students know the properties of substances can change when the substances are mixed, cooled, or heated.

1 **What happens to a liquid if you freeze it?**

   A It changes into a gas.

   B It changes into a solid.

   C It melts.

   D Nothing happens.

2 **This picture shows the Sun shining after it rained.**

What will happen to the puddle?

   A It will boil.

   B It will evaporate.

   C It will freeze.

   D Nothing will happen.

Where in the WORLD is WATER?

Did you know that water covers most of Earth? It has three forms.

Water

Water can be a solid, a liquid, or a gas.

gas

solid

liquid

Solid Water

Water is solid when it is frozen. You can cut it into different shapes.

▲ ice sculpture

Liquid Water

Liquid water fills rivers, lakes, and all the oceans of the world. It falls from the sky as rain.

▲ lake

Water as a Gas

When water boils, it changes from a liquid to a gas. The gas goes into the air.

▲ boiling water

I PS I. Materials come in different forms (states), including solids, liquids, and gases.
ELA R I.2.0. Students read and understand grade-level-appropriate material.

Baker

Do you love to make cookies? You could become a baker. A baker makes breads, cookies, cakes, and other food to sell.

Some bakers have their own bakery. Others, work for big companies.

You must understand the science of baking to be a baker. Bakers learn that when different foods are mixed, they can change.

baker

More careers for people who like to mix things up.

chemist

cement truck operator

Reference

▶ This child is using a
magnifying glass.

Science Content Standards

Physical Sciences

I. **Materials come in different forms (states), including solids, liquids, and gases. As a basis for understanding this concept:**
   a. *Students know* solids, liquids, and gases have different properties.
   b. *Students know* the properties of substances can change when the substances are mixed, cooled, or heated.

Life Sciences

2. **Plants and animals meet their needs in different ways. As a basis for understanding this concept:**
   a. *Students know* different plants and animals inhabit different kinds of environments and have external features that help them thrive in different kinds of places.
   b. *Students know* both plants and animals need water, animals need food, and plants need light.
   c. *Students know* animals eat plants or other animals for food and may also use plants or even other animals for shelter and nesting.
   d. *Students know* how to infer what animals eat from the shapes of their teeth (e.g., sharp teeth: eats meat; flat teeth: eats plants).
   e. *Students know* roots are associated with the intake of water and soil nutrients and green leaves are associated with making food from sunlight.

Earth Sciences

3. Weather can be observed, measured, and described. As a basis for understanding this concept:

    a. *Students know* how to use simple tools (e.g., thermometer, wind vane) to measure weather conditions and record changes from day to day and across the seasons.

    b. *Students know* that the weather changes from day to day but that trends in temperature or rain (or snow) tend to be predictable during a season.

    c. *Students know* the sun warms the land, air, and water.

Investigation and Experimentation

4. Scientific progress is made by asking meaningful questions and conducting careful investigations. As a basis for understanding this concept and addressing the content in the other three strands, students should develop their own questions and perform investigations. Students will:

    a. Draw pictures that portray some features of the thing being described.

    b. Record observations and data with pictures, numbers, or written statements.

    c. Record observations on a bar graph.

    d. Describe the relative position of objects by using two references (e.g., above and next to, below and left of).

    e. Make new observations when discrepancies exist between two descriptions of the same object or phenomenon.

Recycle

It is important to recycle so we have clean air, water, and land.

▲ To help take care of Earth, recycle as much as you can.

▲ When you see this symbol on something, you can recycle the object.

▲ You can use things more than one time.

Clean Up

We need to keep workplaces clean.
Put things where they belong.

▲ It is important to wash your hands.

▲ If something breaks, do not touch it. Let an adult clean up the broken pieces.

◀ Wear a smock or apron so you do not get paint on your clothes.

Care of Plants

Taking care of plants helps you learn about their needs.

▲ Put plants in a sunny place.

▶ Give plants plenty of water.

Care of Animals

Taking care of animals helps you learn about their needs.

▶ Give animals a safe place to live.

▶ Be kind to pets. Handle them with care.

▶ Give pets food and water.

▶ Do not touch wild animals. They might bite, sting, or scratch you.

▶ Do not touch things in places where wild animals live.

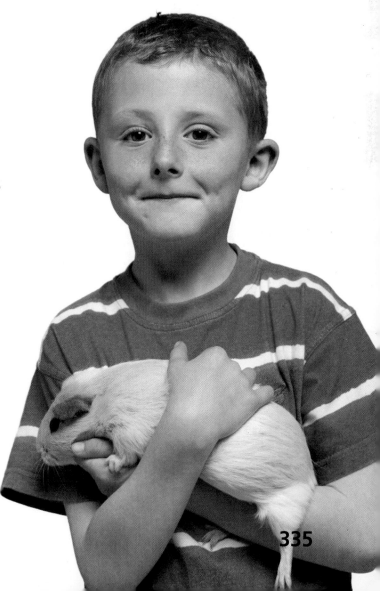

Use a Bar Graph

You can use a bar graph to organize data. The title of the graph tells you the topic of what you are recording. The shaded bars tell you how much of each thing there is.

What was the class's favorite fruit?

Favorite Fruits

Try It

Make your own bar graph to show your class's favorite fruits.

How to Measure

You can use objects to measure. Line up the objects and count them. Use objects that are alike. They must be the same size.

▲ This string is about 8 paper clips long.

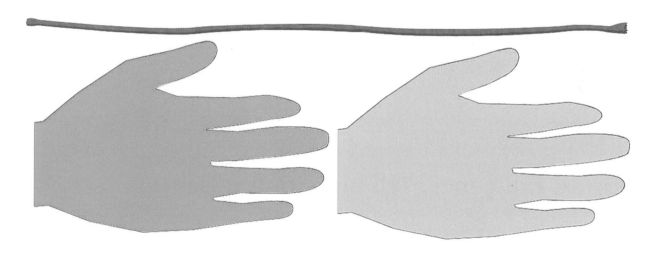

▲ This string is about 2 hands long.

Try It

Measure some string. Tell how you did it.

Measure in Centimeters

You can use a ruler to measure solids. You can use centimeters (cm). This is called a unit of measurement.

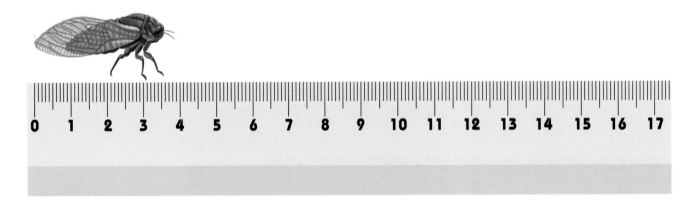

▲ You can measure this fly in centimeters. Line up the end of the fly with the 0 on the ruler. The fly is about 4 centimeters long. This is written as 4 cm.

Try It

Measure the pencil. Tell how long it is.

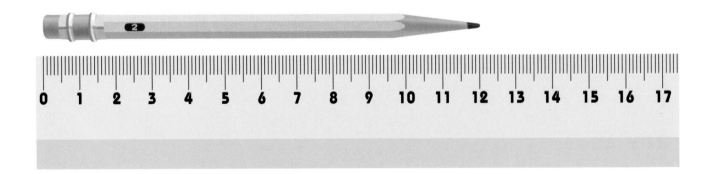

Measure in Inches

You can use inches (in.) to measure, too.
This toy is 3 inches, or 3 in., long.

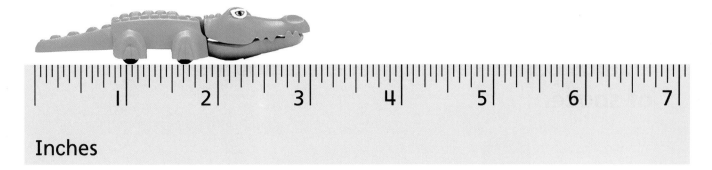

Inches

You can predict how long something is.
When you predict, you guess the length.
Then you can use a ruler to measure it.

Try It

Predict how long
each object is.
Then use a ruler to
measure the objects.

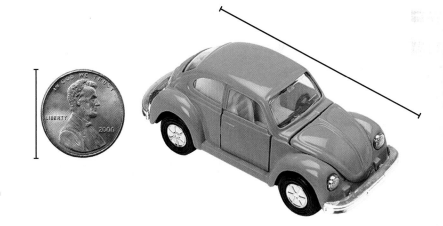

Object	Predict	Measure
penny	about ___ in.	___ in.
toy car	about ___ in.	___ in.

You can use a measuring cup to measure liquids. A measuring cup measures volume. Volume is the amount of space a liquid takes up. Liquids can take up different amounts of space.

Try It

1. Find a container. Predict how much orange juice it can hold.

2. Fill the container with orange juice. Measure the juice in cups. Was your prediction right?

Use a Balance

A balance measures mass. It lets you compare the mass of two different objects.

Place one object on each side of the balance. The object that has more mass will make that side of the balance go down. The object with less mass will go up.

Try It

Place two objects on a balance. Which has more mass?

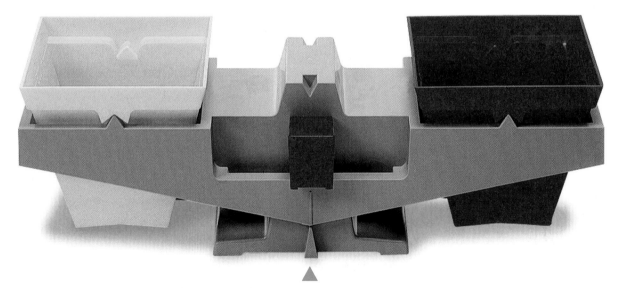

Before you compare masses, make sure the arrow points to the line.

Use a Scale

A scale measures weight. You can measure weight in pounds (lbs). You can measure the weight of fruits and vegetables. You can measure your weight, too.

Try It

1. What is your weight? First predict your weight. Then use a scale to measure it.

2. Every month, measure your weight. Record it in a chart. See how your weight changes as you grow.

Use a Thermometer

A thermometer measures temperature. There is liquid inside the thermometer. When it gets warmer, the liquid moves up. When it gets cooler, the liquid moves down.

Try It

Which thermometer shows a warmer temperature? How can you tell?

A thermometer has marks with numbers. The marks show degrees Fahrenheit and degrees Celsius.

Read this thermometer in degrees Fahrenheit. Look at the numbers on the left side. Find the number where the liquid ends.

degrees Fahrenheit —————— °F °C —————— degrees Celsius

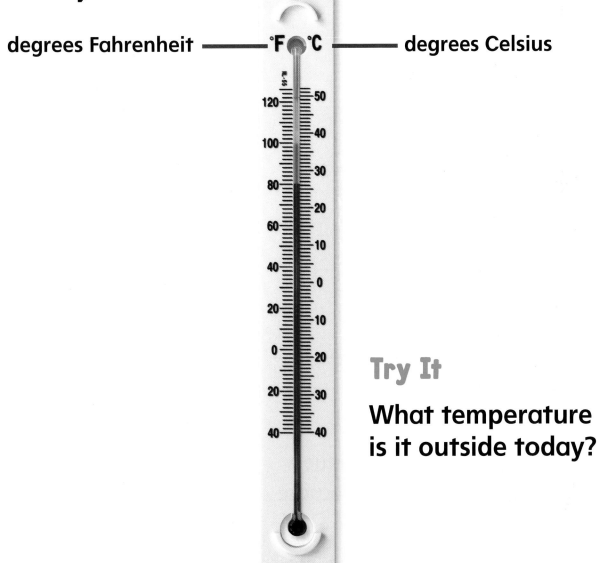

Try It

What temperature is it outside today?

Use Weather Tools

You can use weather tools to measure the weather.

▶ A thermometer tells you how hot or cool the air is.

▲ A rain gauge tells you how much rain falls. It has a ruler to measure the amount of rain in the jar.

Some weather tools help measure wind.

▲ A wind vane tells which way the wind blows.

▶ An anemometer measures how fast the wind blows. It tells the speed of the wind.

Try It

Use a rain gauge. Measure how much rain falls on two rainy days.

Use a Clock

A clock measures time.

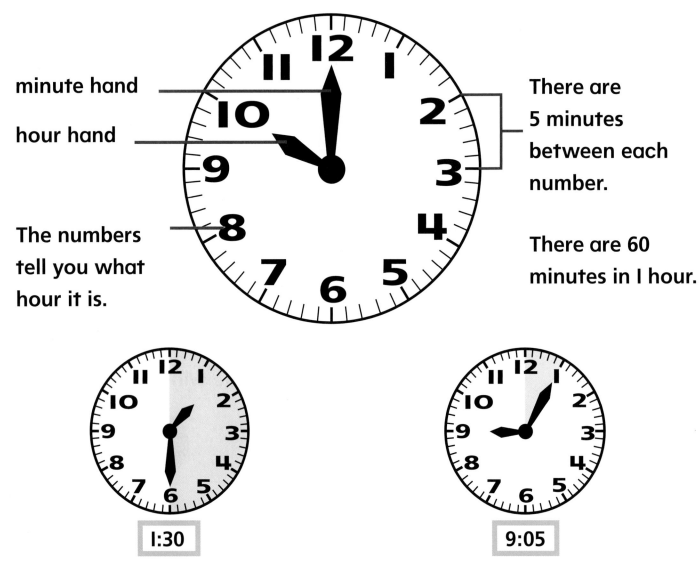

minute hand

hour hand

The numbers tell you what hour it is.

There are 5 minutes between each number.

There are 60 minutes in 1 hour.

1:30

30 minutes after 1 o'clock

9:05

5 minutes after 9 o'clock

Try It

Predict how long you sleep each night. Then use a clock to find out.

Use a Hand Lens

A hand lens makes objects seem larger. Scientists use them to get a closer look at objects.

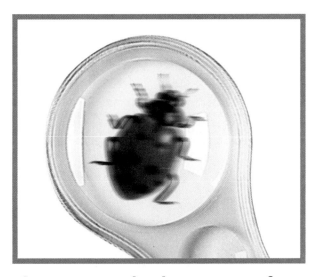

First, move the lens away from the object. Stop when the object looks fuzzy.

Next, move the lens a little closer to the object. Stop when the object looks clear.

Try It

1. Observe each bug here. Use a hand lens.

2. How many legs do you see on the bugs?

3. What else can you see?

Use a Computer

You can use a computer to get information. The Internet is a way to get a lot of information. It links your computer to other computers far away.

▲ When using a computer, make sure an adult knows what you are working on.

Try It

Use the Internet. Learn more about science in your world @ www.macmillanmh.com

Glossary

A

adaptation An adaptation is a special feature that helps an animal stay alive in its habitat. (page 107)

B

balance A balance can be used to measure mass. (page 249)

birds Birds are a group of animals that have feathers. Birds lay eggs. (page 67)

boiling When a liquid gets enough heat, it boils. Boiling can change a liquid to a gas. (page 295)

C

carnivore A carnivore is an animal that eats only other animals. (page 84)

351

cooling Cooling means to take heat away. (page 303)

compare Compare means to see how things are alike and different. You can use a Venn diagram to compare two things. (page 70)

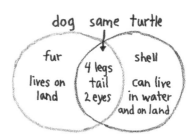

communicate Communicate means to write, draw, or tell your ideas to others. You can use a word web to communicate your ideas. (page 110)

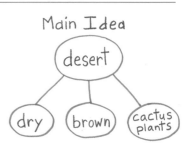

classify Classify means to group things that are alike. (page 11)

D

dissolve Dissolve means to completely mix into a liquid. (page 309)

draw a conclusion To draw a conclusion means to use what you observe to explain what happens. (page 18)

E

energy Energy gives plants and animals the power to do things. (page 36)

evaporate When a liquid evaporates, it changes from a liquid to a gas. When water is heated, some water evaporates, or goes into the air as gas. (page 294)

F

fall Fall is the season after summer. (page 220)

fins Fins help fish swim in water. (page 76)

food chain A food chain shows the order in which living things get the food they need. (page 130)

forest A forest is a place where there are a lot of trees. (page 108)

freeze When you freeze a liquid, it turns into a solid. (page 300)

G

gas Gas is a state of matter that spreads out to fill all the space of whatever it is in. (page 270)

gills Gills help fish take in air from the water. (page 76)

grassland A grassland is a dry place with a lot of grass. (page 106)

H

habitat A habitat is the place where plants and animals get what they need to live.(page 28)

herbivore A herbivore is an animal that eats only plants. (page 82)

I

insect Insects are animals that have three body parts and six legs. (page 69)

L

leaves Leaves use sunlight and air to make food. (page 44)

liquid A liquid is a state of matter. Liquids flow and take the shape of whatever they are in. (page 262)

make a model When you make a model, you make something to show how something looks. (page 87)

mammals Mammals are a group of animals with hair or fur. Most mammals give birth to their young. (page 67)

mass Mass is how much matter is in an object. (page 248)

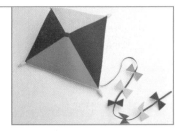

matter Matter is what all things are made up of. (page 247)

measure Measure means to find out the size or amount of something. (page 250)

melting Melting means to change from a solid to a liquid. (page 292)

mixture A mixture is two or more different things put together. (page 308)

N

nutrients Nutrients help a plant grow. (page 46)

O

observe When you observe, you see, hear, taste, touch, or smell to find out about things. (page 30)

Rose	
See	The rose is red.
touch	The flower is smooth.
Smell	The rose smells sweet.

ocean An ocean is salty water that is very large and deep. (page 116)

omnivore An omnivore eats both plants and animals. (page 131)

plants Plants are living things. (page 26)

pond A pond is a small body of fresh water. (page 114)

pollen Pollen is powder inside a flower that makes seeds. (page 123)

predict Predict means to use what you know to tell what will happen. (page 160)

properties Properties are how something looks, feels, smells, or tastes. Color, size, and shape are also properties. (page 246)

put things in order To put things in order means to tell what comes first, next, and last. (page 296)

R

rain gauge A rain gauge measures how much rain falls. (page 173)

record data When you record data, you write down information. You can keep track of the information that you have found. (page 200)

reptiles Reptiles are a group of animals that have dry skin covered with scales. (page 68)

roots Roots take in water and nutrients from the soil. They also help plants stay in the ground. (page 46)

season A season is a time of year. Winter, spring, summer, and fall are the four seasons of the year. (page 196)

shelter A shelter is a place where an animal can be safe. (page 75)

solid A solid is a state of matter that has a shape of its own. (page 254)

spring Spring is the season after winter. (page 204)

states of matter States of matter are the forms of matter. They are solid, liquid, and gas. (page 247)

summer Summer is the season after spring. (page 212)

Sun The Sun is a star. Energy from the Sun heats Earth. (page 165)

temperature Temperature is how cold or warm the air is. (page 158)

texture How an object feels is its texture. Solids might feel smooth or rough. (page 257)

thermometer A thermometer measures the temperature of air and water. (page 173)

water vapor Water vapor is water that goes up into the air. (page 166)

weather Weather is what the air and sky are like each day. (page 156)

wind Wind is moving air. (page 159)

wind vane A wind vane shows the direction of the wind. (page 173)

winter Winter is the coldest season. (page 196)

Credits

Royalty-Free/CORBIS. 136-137: (bkgd) Daryl Benson/Masterfile. 137: (tr) Photodisc/Getty Images; (br) KENT, BRECK P./Animals Animals. 138: Creatas/PunchStock. 139: (t) Sarkis Images/Alamy; (cr) AGE Fotostock/SuperStock. 140-141: AGE Fotostock/SuperStock. 141: (tl) Charles Krebs/Getty Images; (tr) Emilio Ereza/Alamy; (tc) Digital Vision Ltd. 142: WILLIAM ERVIN/SCIENCE PHOTO LIBRARY. 143: (cl) Len Villano/SuperStock; (cr) Steve Dunwell/Index Stock Imagery; (b) Dwight R. Kuhn Photography. 144: (tr) Nicole Duplaix/Getty Images; (br) imagebroker/Alamy. 146: Dan Suzio/Photo Researchers, Inc. 147: (tr)B. RUNK/S. SCHOENBERGER/Grant Heilman Photography; (br) Joel Sartore/Getty Images; (bc) Photodisc/Getty Images. 148: (tr) Thinkstock/Alamy; (br) Bernd Obermann/CORBIS. 149: Robert Glusic/Getty Images. 151-152: Mitsushi Okada/Picture Quest. 152: (tr) Tom Bean/Getty Images; (cr) Stephen Simpson/Getty Images; (br) J.A. Kraulis/Masterfile. 154-155: Tom Bean/Getty Images. 156: (bl) George D. Lepp/Photo Researchers, Inc.; (br) Royalty-Free/CORBIS. 157: (tl) Brand X Pictures/PunchStock; (bl) Robert Brenner/Photo Edit; (br) Rob Casey/Getty Images. 158: (bl) Comstock Images/Alamy; (br) Flynn Larsen/zefa/CORBIS. 159: Terry Qing/Getty Images. 160: David Young-Wolff/Photo Edit. 161: Michael Newman/Photo Edit. 162-163: Stephen Simpson/Getty Images. 164-165: Royalty-Free/CORBIS. 165: J. Luke/Photolink/Getty Images. 167: Altrendo Images/Getty Images. 168: David Young-Wolff/Photo Edit. 169: Photodisc/Getty Images. 170-171: J.A. Kraulis/Masterfile. 172: David Young-Wolff/Photo Edit. 173: (tr bkgd) Taxi/Getty Images; (cl) Tony Freeman/Photo Edit; (cl bkgd) F. Schussler/PhotoLink/Getty Images; (br) Don Farrall/Getty Images; (br bkgd) PhotoLink/Getty Images. 174: Digital Vision/Getty Images. 176: Ellen B. Senisi/The Image Works. 178: NOAA. 179: NASA. 180: ChromaZone Images/Index Stock Imagery. 181: H. van den Heuvel/zefa/CORBIS. 182: Christina Kennedy/Photo Edit. 183: Alan Oddie/Photo Edit. 184: Enigma/Alamy. 185: PhotoLink/Getty Images. 186: (bl) David Frazier/The Image Works; (br) David Young-Wolff/Photo Edit. 187: Jack Sullivan/Alamy. 189: Mitsushi Okada/Picture Quest. 191-192: Brand X Pictures/PunchStock. 192: (tr) Chung Sung Jun/Getty Images; (tcr) Steve Satushek/Getty Images; (bcr) Left Lane Productions/CORBIS; (br) Ariel Skelley/CORBIS. 194-195: Chung Sung Jun/Getty Images. 195: (tr) David Muench/CORBIS; (br) Mike Powell/Getty Images. 196: © 2005 Jeff Schultz/AlaskaStock.com. 196-197: PCL/Alamy. 198: (tr) George Bryce/Animals Animals; (b) Joe McDonald/CORBIS. 199: Photodisc Red/Getty Images. 201: Patrick J. Endres/Alaskaphotographics.com. 202-203: Steve Satushek/Getty Images. 204: blickwinkel/Alamy. 205: Alan Levenson/Alamy. 206: Photowood Inc./CORBIS. 207: Steve Maslowski/Photo Researchers, Inc. 208: David Sanger Photography/Alamy. 208-209: AGE Fotostock/SuperStock. 210-211: Left Lane Productions/CORBIS. 211: Digital Vision/PunchStock. 212: Myrleen Ferguson Cate/Photo Edit. 213: (tr) Paul Gapper/Alamy; (bl) Cary Anderson/Aurora/IPN Stock. 215: (t) SuperStock/AGE Fotostock; (b) Larry Prosor/SuperStock.

216: (cl) Mary Kate Denny/Photo Edit; (cr) Richard Hutchings/ Photo Edit. 217: Comstock/PunchStock. 218-219: Ariel Skelley/CORBIS. 219: (l) Frank Blackburn / Alamy; (r) Galen Rowell/CORBIS; (cl) Matthew Ward/Dorling Kindersley; (cr) Ed Reschke/Peter Arnold, Inc. 220: (bl) Phil Schermeister/National Geographic Image Collection; (br) Jeff Foott/Picture Quest. 221: (bl) oote boe/Alamy; (br) Damian P. Gadal/Alamy. 222: Stock Connection/Alamy. 223: Visions of America, LLC/Alamy. 225: Bill Varie/Alamy. 226: (tl) Richard Hutchings/Photo Edit; (tr) Blend Images/SuperStock; (bl) Mike Powell/Getty Images; (br) Dale Durfee/Getty Images. 227: Richard Hutchings/Photo Edit. 228: Blend Images/SuperStock. 229: Mike Powell/Getty Images. 230: Dale Durfee/Getty Images. 231: (tl) Richard Hutchings/Photo Edit; (tr) Blend Images/SuperStock; (bl) Mike Powell/Getty Images; (br) Dale Durfee/Getty Images. 232: (tcl) Photowood Inc. /CORBIS; (tcr) Joe McDonald/CORBIS; (bl) Jeff Foott/Picture Quest; (br) Phil Schermeister/National Geographic Image Collection. 233: (tl) George Bryce/Animals Animals; (bc) Brand X Pictures/PunchStock. 237: (tr) Corbis/Picture Quest; (cr) Ron Niebrugge/Alamy; (br) Royalty-Free/CORBIS. 238: (tr) MIKE BERGER/JIM REED PHOTOGRAPHY/SCIENCE PHOTO LIBRARY; (bl) Digital Vision/Getty Images; (br) Dennis MacDonald/Alamy. 239: Stock Connection/Picture Quest. 241-242: eStock Photo/Alamy. 242:(tcr) David Muench/CORBIS; (bcr) Steve Murez/Getty Images; (br) Robert Harding Picture Library Ltd/Alamy. 245: (tr) Jules Frazier/Getty Images. 246: Andy Crawford/Dorling Kindersley. 246-247: J.Silver/SuperStock. 247: Dorling Kindersley. 252-253: David Muench/CORBIS. 260-261: Steve Murez/Getty Images. 262: Craig C. Sheumaker/Panoramic Images. 264: (tl) Michael Pohuski/Getty Images; (tr) Sally Ullman/FoodPix; (tc) Digital Vision/Getty Images; (bl) Peter Walton/Index Stock Imagery; (bc) MARTYN F. CHILLMAID/SCIENCE PHOTO LIBRARY; (br) graficart.net/Alamy. 265: Jim Sugar/CORBIS. 266: Michael O'Neill/Grant Heilman Photography. 268-269: Robert Harding Picture Library Ltd/Alamy. 270: Royalty-Free/CORBIS. 271: (bc) David Young-Wolff/Alamy; (cr) José Fuste Raga/zefa/CORBIS. 273: Brand X Pictures/PunchStock. 276-277: Andre Jenny/Alamy. 278: Digital Vision/PunchStock. 279: Elizabeth Whiting & Associates/Alamy. 280: Grace/zefa/CORBIS. 281: P. I. Productions/SuperStock. 282: Sally Ullman/FoodPix. 283: eStock Photo/Alamy. 287-288: Steven Needham/Envision. 288: (tr) Douglas Peebles Photography/Alamy; (cr) Walter Bibikow/Getty Images; (br) Garry Black/Masterfile. 290-291: Douglas Peebles Photography/Alamy. 292: (cl) Richard Cummins/SuperStock; (br) Burke/Triolo Productions/Getty Images. 293: (tr) Stockbyte Silver/Alamy; (b) Gregor M. Schmid/CORBIS. 295: Omni Photo/Index Stock Imagery. 296: (c bkgd) Daniel Barillot/Masterfile; (c) C Squared Studios/Getty Images. 297: (t) ScottBarrow, Inc./SuperStock; (br) Photodisc/Getty Images. 298: Walter Bibikow/Getty Images. 306: Garry Black/Masterfile. 313: foodfolio/Alamy. 316-317: C Squared Studios/Getty Images. 318: Dennis Gray/Cole Group/

Getty Images. 319: Jan Oswald/Getty Images. 320: Mitch Hrdlicka/Getty Images. 321: Paul Poplis/Envision. 322: (tr) Stockbyte Silver/Alamy; (cr) Francisco Cruz/SuperStock; (br) Omni Photo/Index Stock Imagery. 323: Christina Kennedy/Photo Edit. 326: Jonathan Andrew/CORBIS. 327: (tr) Steve Kaufman/CORBIS; (cr) Emma Lee/Life File/Getty Images; (br) K. Hackenberg/zefa/Corbis. 328: (tr) Rosenfeld Images Ltd./Photo Researchers, Inc.; (bl) RubberBall/SuperStock; (br) Justin Kase/Alamy. 329: Ariel Skelley/CORBIS. 332: Photodisc/Getty Images. 333: (tl) Michael Newman/Photo Edit; (bl) Myrleen Ferguson Cate/Photo Edit. 334: (tr) James Baigrie/Getty Images; (br) Doug Menuez/Getty Images. 335: (tr) Photodisc Collection/Getty Images; (bl) GK Hart/Vikki Hart/Getty Images; (br) Stockbyte/Getty Images. 336: Jules Frazier/Getty Images. 343: (tr) foodfolio/Alamy; (b) Photodisc/Getty Images. 344: (l) Photodisc/Getty Images; (cr) Paul Thomas/Getty Images. 347: (l) Bonnie Sue Rauch/Photo Researchers, Inc.; (r) Tony Freeman/Photo Edit. 349: Photodisc/Getty Images. 350: Lukas Creter/Getty Images. 351: (t to b) Nigel J. Dennis/Photo Researchers, Inc.; FLIP DE NOOYER/FOTO NATURA/Minden Pictures; Omni Photo/Index Stock Imagery; Bruce Coleman Brakefield/Alamy. 352: (t to b) Brand X Pictures/Getty Images; Royalty-Free/CORBIS; Brand X Pictures/Getty Images. 353: (t to b) Jeff Foott/Picture Quest; Stockdisc/Getty Images; Art Wolfe/Getty Images. 354: (t to b) Royalty-Free/CORBIS; Stockdisc/Getty Images; Jeremy Woodhouse/Masterfile; Robert Marien/Index Stock Imagery; Raymond Mendez/Animals Animals. 355: (t to b) McDonald Wildlife Photography/Animals Animals; Dorling Kindersley. 356: (t to b) Burke/Triolo Productions/Getty Images; Neil Fletcher & Matthew Ward/Getty Images; Siede Preis/Getty Images; David Fleetham/Getty Images; Steve Dunwell/Index Stock Imagery; imagebroker/Alamy; David Young-Wolff/Photo Edit. 357: (t to b) Andy Crawford/Dorling Kindersley; Dan Suzio Photography; John Kaprielian/Photo Researchers, Inc.; Stock Connection/Alamy. 358: (t to b) Daniel J Cox/Getty Images; Photowood Inc./CORBIS; Super Stock/AGE Fotostock; J.Luke/Photolink/Getty Images; Comstock Images/Alamy; Stock Connection/Alamy. 359: (t to b) Royalty-Free/CORBIS; Terry Qing/Getty Images; Don Farrall/Getty Images; © 2005 Jeff Schultz/AlaskaStock.com.

All Illustrations are by Macmillan/McGraw Hill (MMH) except as noted below:

22-23: Mike Reed. 45: Bob Masheris. 47: Sam Tomasello. 59: Linda Bittner. 62-63: Larry Reinhart. 83-84: Kathleen McKeehen. 99: Linda Bittner. 102-103: Ron Broda. 130-131: Patrick Gnan. 142: Patrick Gnan. 145: Linda Bittner. 152-153: Sue Williams. 175: Jean Wisenbaugh. 192-193: Melanie Hall. 195: Jean Wisenbaugh. 209: Jean Wisenbaugh. 214-215: Jean Wisenbaugh. 235: Ralph Canaday. 242-243: Marisol Sarrazin. 272: Sam Tomasello. 283: Judy Stead. 285: Burgundy Beam. 288-289: Sally Jo Vitsky. 325: Burgundy Beam.

Acknowledgments

"Giraffes" from *The Llama Who Had No Pajama: 100 Favorite Poems* by Mary Ann Hoberman. Copyright © 1973 by Mary Ann Hoberman, reprinted by permission of Harcourt, Inc.

"Our World" from *101 Science Poems & Songs for Young Learners* by Meish Goldish. Copyright © 1996 by Meish Goldish. Published by Scholastic, Incorporated. All rights reserved.

"Popcorn Hop" from *Kindergarten Kids* by Stephanie Calmenson. Text Copyright © 2005 by Stephanie Calmenson. Published by HarperCollins Publishers. All rights reserved.

"Sudden Storm" from *The Sparrow Bush* by Elizabeth Coatsworth. Text Copyright © 1966 by W.W. Norton & Company. All rights reserved.

"Sunflakes" from *Country Pie* by Frank Asch. Copyright © 1979 by Frank Asch. Published by Greenwillow Books. All rights reserved.

"To Be a Clover" from *Out in the Dark and Daylight* by Aileen Fisher. Text Copyright © 1980 by Aileen Fisher. Published by Harper & Row Publishers. All rights reserved.

"Tommy" from *Bronzeville Boys and Girls* by Gwendolyn Brooks. Text Copyright © 1965 by Gwendolyn Brooks. Published by Harper & Row, Incorporated. All rights reserved.